ALASKA

Anderson Island

Prince William Sd.

Kamchatka

Aleutian Islands

Nootka Island

NORTH AMERICA

HAWAIIAN ISLANDS

PACIFIC OCEAN

SOUTH AMERICA

Solomon Islands

Marquesas Islands

Apr 1, 1774

Fiji

Friendly Islands

Cook Islands

Tahiti

Mar 31, 1769

Easter Island

New Caledonia

Oct 5, 1774

Oct 14, 1773

Norfolk Island

Botany Bay

Oct 1, 1769

Mar 17, 1777

Apr 6, 1770

Jul 1, 1773

Dusky Bay

Queen Charlotte Sd.

Jan 1, 1769

NEW ZEALAND

Christmas Sd.

Cape Horn

Mar 16, 1773

Nov 21, 1774

Jan 1, 1774

Jan 30, 1769

Jan 6, 1775

Feb 1, 1774

Price: $4.50

James Cook
and New Zealand

James Cook and New Zealand

The Voyage of the *Endeavour,* 1768–1771
The Voyage of the *Resolution* and *Adventure,* 1772–1775
The Voyage of the *Resolution* and *Discovery,* 1776–1780

A. Charles Begg

and

Neil C. Begg

A. R. Shearer, Government Printer, Wellington, New Zealand—1970

First Published October 1969
Reprinted February 1970

Layout and design by E. L. Dyne, Government Printing Office, and J. D. Pascoe, Department of Internal Affairs.

Front cover:
James Cook. A portrait painted by Nathaniel Dance in 1776.

Back cover:
Underwater plaque near the place where Cook was killed in Kealakekua Bay, Hawaii.

Frontispiece:
Captain Cook greets the Maoris at Ship Cove in Queen Charlotte Sound, New Zealand. Watercolour drawing by John Webber.

TO CAPTAIN JAMES COOK
and to all those who sailed to New Zealand
under his command

Foreword

THIS book will give its readers—and I hope they will be many—a good idea of the activities of James Cook on the coasts of New Zealand. If they want to know more, they will have to read Cook himself, and Banks, and the writings of the other men who sailed with Cook. They will do well to study the illustrations here given, too, for no voyage before that of the *Endeavour* was so fully and accurately pictured as hers was. The present authors have worked hard on the material in the ordinary way. They have done more than that—and this I find admirable: they have put sweat and acuteness into their field work, have followed their own example in Dusky Sound, have gone out to sea and looked at the coastline as Cook looked, have climbed his hills and taken his charts to the top of them. There is no substitute for this sort of field work in studying the history of discovery. You can go so far with paper, you may write with vividness and point; but in the end, to be safe, you have to go and look. Of course it can be expensive, and even then you may not feel quite safe. Well, if you want to peg your life to absolute certainty, history is hardly a safe pursuit.

As we pursue Cook and the Begg brothers round the coast of our country, and study the drawings so diligently made by Sydney Parkinson and Spöring, we may consider broadly Cook as a discoverer of New Zealand, and the effect on Cook of his discovery. Of course we all know that he was preceded here by the Polynesians, and by Tasman. We infer that amongst the Polynesians there must have been very competent sailors, and we know from the records that Tasman was an extremely competent sailor; but taking only into account the men who kept journals, and thus left records, we can say without injustice that Cook much more than Tasman was the discoverer of the country. True enough, Tasman found it first, and left a scratch on the map to indicate its position, or the position of some of it. Certainly the scratch was good enough as an indication, as far as it went. It was a help to Cook. But Cook, as still another Pacific voyager and New Zealand discoverer, d'Urville, said, created a new era in geographical science. He didn't merely put scratches on maps. Once he had found a coast he clung to it grimly until he had ascertained its full extent, he made a chart that was both full and accurate. Of course (again) he was lucky. He himself belonged to a new era in science. The eighteenth century was one of the great ages of intellectual exploration and technical invention: nautical astronomy and the sextant and the chronometer gave Cook methods and instruments for settling his position and the positions of capes and bays that Tasman had not dreamed of. But there were other sailors in that eighteenth century who did not do much better than Tasman did. The important thing was the character of the man, his obstinate persistence in hanging on—to the North Cape, to Cape Maria van Diemen—till he was sure that in spite of all tempests he had got them down on his chart exactly where they ought to be. At the end of his circumnavigation that chart, as he found out later, was slightly astray in longitude; and we know that it had a few other defects. But there had never been another chart like it in all the history of discovery. There were not many charts as good in all the atlases. And it was the fruit of 6 months' work. Cook did another thing that Tasman did not do: he landed in the country. What he and the nimble-minded Banks noticed and recorded about it and its people, what the scientists recorded about its botany, were the foundations of our ethnography and natural science. Cook's two great watchwords, as you find when you read his journals, were Geography and Navigation: you also find that carried in these words were all manner of other sciences. The new era he belonged to, the new era that he created, had tremendous implications.

While Cook was thus important for New Zealand, New Zealand was important for him. The chart was important for him. He was a hydrographer and marine surveyor. It was on this chart that he perfected his ability at a "running survey", as distinct from the slow (but fast enough) beautifully detailed work he had done, season after season, by triangulation on land as well as careful observation from the sea, in Newfoundland in the mid-1760s. He was a master, but he was still learning. That was a technical matter, and it need not be enlarged on here. He was learning other things as well. He was learning, for instance, how useful New Zealand could be as a base for future Pacific exploration, so that it was to become a pivotal point in his strategy. He was learning, above all, how to get on with a newly found, indigenous people. Tasman didn't help him there. He was extending his knowledge of mankind. But how do you deal with mankind—not the Lords of the Admiralty or the gentlemen of the Royal Society, or British sailors, but Maoris or New Hebrideans or Eskimos or the aborigines of Australia? True, he had got on well with the Tahitians, but the Tahitians had had some experience of Europeans. He knew, more or less, what to expect. At Poverty Bay he did not know what to expect, and as the people came off from different parts of the coast he had his surprises. A humane person he was, he had been told by the President of the Royal Society to be humane, but how did you put humanity into practice? The New Zealand story is interesting. If there was one thing Cook hated, it was killing men. After Poverty Bay and Cape Kidnappers he managed, not quite invariably but almost so, to avoid it. His New Zealand experience was behind that. He had acquired a new skill. He had also acquired for the Maori people a strong regard which is a little difficult to understand, unless we get beneath the surface. He had spent more time in Tahiti, and knew its people better. They had their virtues. They were cousins of the Maori. The Maori did not behave to him with any notable generosity, unseen elsewhere in the Pacific. Yet he speaks of them with an admiration and regard he does not express for other peoples, however highly he might think of individuals among these. He preserved this feeling through his second and third voyages, and it was unaltered by the incident at Grass Cove. The New Zealanders might eat Furneaux's men: he was puzzled rather than outraged. What had gone so seriously wrong? He had the anthropologist's outlook. The New Zealanders are a civilised people, in their own way: as the anthropologist might say, they had their culture-pattern, just as the British sailor had his. Cook could see below the savage surface, he had a sense of savage values, and he could correlate them with his own. It is clear that the Maori people, on their part, had some sense of the stature of the man who had come among them. We have to regret that, confined to the coastline as he was, he did not meet any of the really great chiefs of the time. Nevertheless, his perceptiveness and judgment, however it came about, were not violently at fault. We can deduce from his journals, if we read them attentively, a running survey of his own mind; and we can match Cook's discovery of New Zealand and its people with our discovery of Cook.

There is a great deal more that one is tempted to say; but this is the foreword and not the book. There had never been a chart like this before: yes. There had never been discovery like this before. There had never, in the trade of discovery, been a man like this before. Let it go at that.

J. C. BEAGLEHOLE

London,
July 1969.

Contents

Introduction

Lieutenant Cook awaits fair winds

London Gazette, 19 August 1768

Just over 200 years ago an English newspaper, the *London Gazette*, dated Friday, 19 August 1768, carried arresting headlines over its front-page feature story. 'Secret Voyage' it proclaimed, and then, 'Lieutenant Cook awaits fair winds'. To provoke further interest the editor added a sub-title in smaller but blacker print, 'Search for unknown continent south of the equator'.

The journalist who forwarded the story wrote from Plymouth where His Majesty's Bark *Endeavour* awaited her day of departure. He felt the romance of this exciting voyage into the unknown and believed he could detect an air of mystery. '*Endeavour*', he wrote, 'under its Commander, Lt James Cook, is awaiting fair winds to begin its long Voyage to the Pacific Ocean island of Tahiti to observe, for the Royal Society, the Transit of the planet Venus across the face of the Sun.'

His reporter's eye noted the extensive alterations which had been made to the ship, during the past few months at the Deptford shipyards, and he wondered if all this had been undertaken merely for a scientific study on an island which had recently been discovered and charted by Captain Wallis of the *Dolphin*.

He doubted it. In fact, he maintained that he had 'Certain Information to the contrary'. His doubts should have been dispelled by the denials that the voyage had any other purpose, given to him both by the Lords of the Admiralty and by Lieutenant Cook himself, who had 'brought *Endeavour* to Plymouth only last week'. Despite this, however, his suspicions persisted and he proceeded to give his views as to the real nature of the projected voyage. 'We have reason to believe these Orders are for a Voyage of Discovery, and will carry *Endeavour* to lands far distant in the South Pacific, and even to that vast Continent which is said to be quite as big as Europe and Asia together, and which is now marked on the maps as *Terra Australis Nondum Cognita*.'

One hundred and twenty-six years before this, Abel Tasman had discovered New Zealand and many, including the noted geographer Alexander Dalrymple, considered that it was the northern promontory of a vast continent in the southern seas. Was this the real objective of the *Endeavour's* voyage? He went on, 'Such Orders would no doubt contain instructions to Lt Cook to take for HIS MAJESTY possession of such uninhabited Countries as may be found, and to set up proper marks as first Discoverers and Possessors.'

As a good reporter he was aware of the news value of personal details and he next introduced the men who were embarking on the great adventure. 'Lt Cook is a tall, impressive man with an agreeable modesty. His conversation is lively and intelligent, and in spite of his air of austerity he is well-liked and respected by his men. He has been commended to the Admiralty as a genius, well qualified for great undertakings.'

The ship's company, he pointed out, had been most carefully chosen and contained some very able officers. The First Officer was Lieutenant Zachary Hicks, described as 'an experienced seaman'. Then there was a group who had just returned with Wallis from Tahiti. It included Lieutenant John Gore, Mr Robert Molineux, the master, and his mates, Mr Richard Pickersgill and Mr Charles Clarke. Mr Monkhouse was the surgeon, Mr John Satterly the carpenter, Mr Richard Orton the clerk and Mr Stephen Forward the

Plate 1. *The* Endeavour *ships a heavy sea. Sketch by Sydney Parkinson.*

gunner who was in charge of the *Endeavour's* 12 swivel and 10 carriage guns.

The unnamed crew consisted of a cook, a steward, 2 quartermasters, an armourer, a sailmaker, 3 midshipmen, 41 able seamen, 9 servants and 12 of His Majesty's marines 'to protect the Ship's Complement from attack by savages'.

Illustrating the article, the *London Gazette* carried a plan of the *Endeavour's* decks and hold. She was described as a three-masted Whitby collier, chosen after much deliberation by the Lords of the Admiralty. 'In the manner of all coal-boats, she is exceptionally strongly built with ample space for stowage of stores.'

If the projected voyage was only to increase scientific knowledge the writer admitted that the strong contingent from the Royal Society would permit the appropriate studies to be made. The society 'has been so impressed with the splendid work Lt Cook has already done that it has appointed him as one of their Observers during the Transit of Venus. The other Observer is Mr Charles Green, assistant to the Astronomer Royal.' He drew attention to the scientists and naturalists about to join the ship and noted that they were being led by the brilliant botanist, Mr Banks. 'Mr Banks is paying his own expenses on the Voyage, and also the expenses of his assistants and servants. His second-in-command is Dr Daniel Solander, a knowledgable student of natural history. Mr Alexander Buchan and Mr Sidney Parkinson have been engaged to sketch views and plants.'

The reporter had also uncovered some unusual features of the voyage. He related that Lieutenant Cook was going to take some 'Portable Broth' to prevent 'falling foul to the cursed disease of scurvy' and added in some surprise, 'This truly remarkable concoction is understood to contain a mixture of scurvy grass, marmalade of carrots, syrup of lemons, and other vegetables'. He also thought it would 'be interesting for the Reader to note that milk will be supplied to Officers from a goat which is the very same animal which was carried for that purpose on HIS MAJESTY'S Ship *Dolphin*.'

No doubt the *London Gazette's* article faithfully described the busy scene at Plymouth before the departure of the *Endeavour*. But, though the reporter tried to glimpse the future by piecing together dockyard gossip, he could not know what lay ahead for Lieutenant Cook and his vessel. He concluded his article on a safer note. 'We are confident that all Englishmen will join with us in wishing Lt Cook and his men Favourable Winds and Good Fortune.'

Just one week later, on Friday, 26 August 1768, the *Endeavour* sailed from Plymouth before a fresh north-west breeze. James Cook's first great voyage of exploration had begun (plate 1).

THE FIRST VOYAGE

1   The Southern Continent

*This land looks like being a very beautiful land and
we trust that this is the mainland coast of the unknown
South Land*

Abel Tasman

The inspired reporting in the *London Gazette* was very close to the mark. The Admiralty's sealed orders directed Lieutenant Cook to proceed to Tahiti 'to observe the Passage of the Planet Venus over the Disk of the Sun on the 3rd of June 1769. . . .' After further detailed orders the instructions concluded—'When this Service is perform'd, you are to put to Sea without Loss of Time, and carry into execution the Additional Instructions contained in the inclosed Sealed Packet.'

There was now a note of urgency and the 'Additional Instructions' were explicit. 'You are therefore in Pursuance of His Majesty's Pleasure hereby requir'd and directed to put to Sea with the Bark you Command so soon as the Observation of the Transit of the Planet Venus shall be finished and observe the following Instructions. You are to proceed to the southward in order to make discovery of the Continent above-mentioned until you arrive in the Latitude of 40°, unless you sooner fall in with it. But not having discover'd it or any Evident signs of it in that Run, you are to proceed in search of it to the Westward between the Latitude before mentioned and the Latitude of 35° until you discover it, or fall in with the Eastern side of the Land discover'd by Tasman and now called New Zeland.'

The existence, and the latitude, of New Zealand was known for certain from the reports from Abel Tasman, the Dutch navigator, who mapped the western coast of the country without discovering the strait which separates the islands. Observations during his voyage along the coast in 1642–43 caused geographers to speculate as to whether New Zealand was a northern extension of the large southern continent which they believed must exist to counterbalance the land masses of the northern hemisphere (plate 2).

The Admiralty's orders contained many instructions and suggestions about the exploring of coasts, observing the nature of the soils and minerals, meeting the inhabitants, studying the climate and natural history, and maintaining the health of his crew. They suggested that he should plan his route home by the way he thought 'Most Eligible.' All these things were to be done, 'without Suffering yourself however to be thereby diverted from the Object which you are always to have in View, the Discovery of the Southern Continent so often Mentioned.'

The maps of that time depicted a huge land in the south labelled *Terra Australis Nondum Cognita*—the southern land not yet discovered. Though this may have been true for Europeans, New Zealand had long been known to the Polynesians.

According to Maori tradition Kupe discovered New Zealand over 1,000 years ago. This famous Polynesian voyager ranged the Pacific Ocean in his great canoe and took back to his homeland in Hawaiki details of Tiritiri o te moana—the land that is shrouded by the high mists. The news of an uninhabited land in the direction of the setting sun led to other voyages to New Zealand. The first settlers to follow Kupe's sailing instructions brought no domesticated plants or animals with them and, being dependent upon hunting for food, were attracted to the haunts of the flightless moas which were more numerous in the South Island.

Later, about A.D. 1350, the great fleet set sail from Tahiti for New Zealand. These large ocean-going canoes were able to complete the voyage in less than a fortnight and they carried, in addition

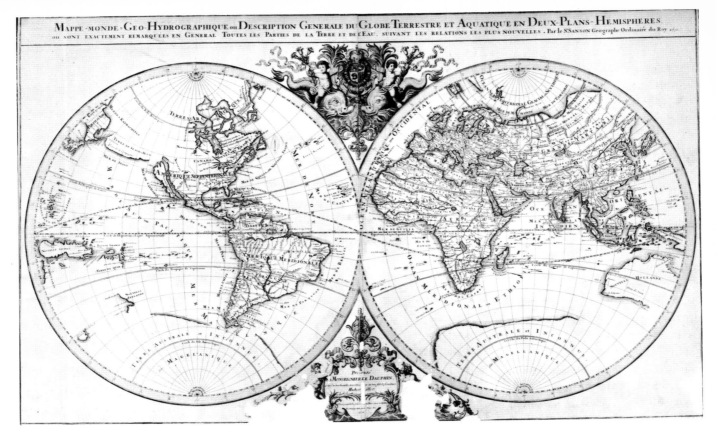

to the food for the journey, cultivable plants, seeds, dogs and rats. The paper mulberry tree which was used for making cloth survived only in the warmest parts of New Zealand, and the tropical plants, such as the sweet potato, taro and yam, were also best suited to the warmer climate of the North Island. These Maori people flourished and multiplied in their new homeland and adapted their way of life to the geography, the climate and the food supplies found under the varying conditions of the North and South Islands. They called the North Island Te Ika a Maui—the fish of Maui—after a legendary figure, half man and half god, who was said to have hauled it up from the sea with an enchanted hook. The South Island was named Te Wai Pounamu after its most valued product pounamu, or greenstone, which was found only in the mountains and gorges of the south, and was laboriously converted into weapons, tools and ornaments of great strength and beauty.

The shell of isolation was cracked by Tasman when he sighted New Zealand on 13 December 1642. The hostile reception given to him by the Maoris drove him away, but his observations and his maps, taken back to the Old World, opened the way for further exploration. It was Tasman's estimation of the latitude of New Zealand that determined the route along which James Cook was directed.

At certain periods of history social and economic pressures increase, opportunities reveal themselves, new methods evolve and knowledge builds on itself until, at a critical moment in time, great discoveries seem almost inevitable. Victor Hugo wrote, 'No army can withstand the strength of an idea whose time has come.' The great men are those who sense the moment, seize the opportunity and translate the ideas into action.

Perhaps the most compelling circumstances in the 1760s which made voyages of exploration seem necessary arose from the political and economic fields. Just as Spain had profited from the vast treasure of silver and gold brought back to Europe as a result of her conquests in Central and South

4

America, so might Britain grow rich from discoveries in the southern seas. Trade and wealth from the only unexplored area in the world would alter the balance of power in Europe. Already Louis-Antoine de Bougainville had sailed from France to take possession of any lands he might discover in the Pacific Ocean.

New opportunities for extended voyages of exploration stemmed from the work of a quiet Scottish naval surgeon, James Lind who, in 1753, wrote a treatise on the prevention and treatment of 'the scurvy'. Up till this time scurvy had been a major barrier to voyages of long duration. The application of Lind's theories and techniques might provide a way in which scurvy could be held at bay for the months and years necessary for the exploration of the furthest parts of the world.

Improved methods of navigation were evolving during the second half of the eighteenth century. Britain, as a maritime nation, depended on their accuracy both for her trade and for her defence. Hadley's sextant was used widely and measured latitude, as distance north or south of the equator, with some precision. More difficult was the estimation of longitude, the distance east or west from a chosen meridian. By the late 1760s, however, two promising methods had reached the testing stage. That of Dr Nevil Maskelyne depended on lunar observations and the use of *The Nautical Almanac*, first published in 1766, the other was based on the first accurate marine clock or 'watch-machine' developed by John Harrison in 1759.

With the ability to pin-point geographic features more accurately came the need to record these positions for the use of subsequent visitors. James Cook acquired the art of mapping while surveying the dangerous waters of the St. Lawrence River before the battle of Quebec, and later practised it around the intricate and treacherous coastlines of Labrador and Newfoundland.

Scientific knowledge was also growing rapidly in other spheres. Almost as important as charting the seas was the system of classification of plants which was devised by Carl Linnaeus, the Swedish botanist, in the middle years of the eighteenth century. As a result botanists, many of them his students, scoured the world collecting, describing and recording new species. In this exciting development British scientists were in the future to play a full part; and one young man, a Fellow of the Royal Society of London called Joseph Banks, had immediate ambitions.

It was, in fact, the Royal Society which initiated the action which led to this voyage. The society wrote a 'memorial' to King George III in February 1768, stating—'That the passage of the Planet Venus over the Disc of the Sun, which will happen on the 3rd of June in the year 1769, is a Phaenomenon that must, if the same be accurately observed in proper places, contribute greatly to the improvement of Astronomy on which navigation so much depends.' King George enthusiastically supported the proposals and in March 1768, placed £4,000 at the disposal of the Royal Society and ordered the Navy to provide ships for the transport of the astronomers.

Three observation points were necessary, two in the northern hemisphere and one in the southern. Captain Samuel Wallis had recently returned from a voyage round the world in the *Dolphin* and was able to report that he had discovered an island in the Pacific Ocean well-suited for an observatory, where water, wood and provisions could be obtained in abundance. It was decided that King George's Island, known to its inhabitants as Tahiti, would be a suitable place for the southern observation point.

The Royal Society thought that Alexander Dalrymple, a famous geographer, would be suitable for the command of the expedition but the idea of a civilian commander was 'totally repugnant' to the Lords of the Admiralty. Instead they chose James Cook. It was as if his whole life had been a preparation for this voyage. He had learned his seamanship before the mast in the hard school of the North Sea coal ships before he joined the Navy. In the Royal Navy his 'genius and capacity' for marine surveying and his 5 years of practical experience as an hydrographer made him the logical choice for command of the expedition. He was appointed at the beginning of May 1768, and commissioned as a lieutenant on 25 May 1768, being directed to use the utmost dispatch in getting his ship to sea. The Royal Society was well pleased with the appointment for it had formed a high opinion of his ability as a result of a paper on an eclipse of the sun in 1766 which he had prepared. The society appointed him as one of its official observers of the transit of Venus at Tahiti. The other observer was to be Mr Charles Green, assistant to the Astronomer Royal.

In the selection of a suitable vessel the Lords of the Admiralty had wasted little time. A round-bowed, deep-waisted, Whitby collier would seem

Plate 3. *Joseph Banks. Painting by Sir Joshua Reynolds.*

They have got a fine library of Natural History; they have all sorts of machines for catching and preserving insects; all kinds of nets, trawls, drags and hooks for coral fishing, they have even a curious contrivance of a telescope, by which, put into the water, you can see the bottom at a great depth, where it is clear . . . besides there are many people whose sole business is to attend them for this very purpose. They have two painters and draughtsmen . . . in short Solander assured me this expedition would cost Mr Banks £10,000.'

Banks's suite consisted of Dr Daniel Carl Solander, who had studied medicine and natural history under Linnaeus, with Herman Spöring, a fellow Swede, as secretary, two artists and four servants. The inclusion of the artists showed that Banks was anxious to obtain a comprehensive pictorial record of the voyage.

The artists had several important functions. The detailed drawings of plants, fishes and birds was to be the specialised task of Sydney Parkinson. Alexander Buchan's work included figure drawing depicting the native inhabitants, their clothing, their implements and weapons, their canoes and their environment. But his chief responsibility was landscape painting which would include the harbours, hills and villages. In addition, he would draw the topographical features of the lands found. It must be remembered that navigation was so inexact, before Cook, that explorers had great difficulty in determining whether an island, for instance, was a new discovery or merely wrongly positioned on the map. An exact drawing of the geographical features would be of great assistance in future identification. In addition, a sketch of the entrance of a harbour would be valuable to any who subsequently wished to enter it.

By 26 August 1768, Cook had completed all preparations for departure and, with fair winds, the *Endeavour* set sail from Plymouth for the South Seas. After calling at Madeira, Rio de Janeiro and Tierra del Fuego, Cape Horn was rounded with unexpected ease and the course set for Tahiti. Cook was able to hold a course more westerly than previous circumnavigators but he found no evidence of a Southern Continent.

The *Endeavour* sailed into Wallis's anchorage at Matavai Bay in Tahiti on 13 April 1769, leaving ample time to set up the observatory on shore (plates 4 and 5). The natives were friendly and courteous and the free and easy island life, with plentiful food, was doubly attractive to the visitors

to have been an unlikely choice and it is quite possible that they were influenced in this by its future commander. They bought the *Earl of Pembroke*, a cat-built bark of 368 tons and nearly 4 years old, for £2,307 5s. 6d. It was renamed the *Endeavour Bark* and moved to Deptford shipyards for fitting out for foreign service.

At this late stage the scope of the proposed expedition was extended by the unexpected and enthusiastic participation of a wealthy, young amateur botanist, Joseph Banks (plate 3). In 1766, at the age of 23 years, he was made a Fellow of the Royal Society and in the same year a desire for adventure and the furtherance of his studies had taken him to Labrador and Newfoundland. When he heard of the preparations being made for a voyage to the Pacific Ocean he sought permission to join the *Endeavour*. Confident of gaining the approval of the Admiralty he applied his wealth and influence to advancing his plans. Banks had lavish ideas, details of which were revealed by a fellow botanist, John Ellis, in a letter to Carl Linnaeus in Uppsala. 'No people ever went to sea better fitted out for the purpose of Natural History.

Plate 4 (above). *"A view of part of the West side of Georges Island taken from the Ship at Anchor in Royal Bay." By Lieutenant J. Cook, 1769. At the left the observatory may be seen near the tip of Point Venus, on the right is One Tree Hill overlooking Matavai Bay.*

Plate 5 (right). *Matavai Bay today, looking over One Tree Hill towards Point Venus. The* Endeavour *was anchored within the shelter of the encircling coral reef.*

after the rigours of the long sea voyage. Charting, trading, botanising and building the appropriately named 'Fort Venus' made the time pass quickly until 3 June 1769, when the transit of Venus was observed in perfect weather conditions. Green, Solander and Cook made the observations which should have been successful, but Cook noted in his journal—'we very distinctly saw an Atmosphere or dusky shade round the body of the Planet which very much disturbed the times of the Contacts', and the results differed 'much more than could be expected.'

Before leaving Tahiti Cook befriended a native named Tupaia who was familiar with the Polynesian dialects and claimed to know more than a hundred South Sea islands. He was embarked as interpreter and pilot and took with him, as servant, a little native boy called Taiata. The *Endeavour* sailed from Tahiti on 13 July 1769, and Cook explored some of the islands of the Society group. Following his additional instructions he continued in his search, driving the *Endeavour* south to the

40th parallel of latitude before the equinoctial gales forced him to sail west towards the setting sun. By the spring of 1769 his calculations showed that he had followed the Admiralty's instructions to the letter and, according to Tasman's map, should be approaching New Zealand. Indeed, an increase in the number of seals and birds, pieces of seaweed and floating wood, sudden variable squalls of wind and a change in the colour of the water all seemed to indicate that land was near.

On 29 September 1769, Sydney Parkinson, the talented young artist, wrote in his diary, 'The captain apprehended that we were near land, and promised one gallon of rum to the man who should first discover it by day, and two if he discovered it by night; also, that part of the coast of the said land should be named after him.' Thus encouraged, interest in the long-awaited landfall mounted and speculation was rife.

Banks described the scene in the great cabin a few days later. 'Now do I wish that our freinds in England could by the assistance of some magical

7

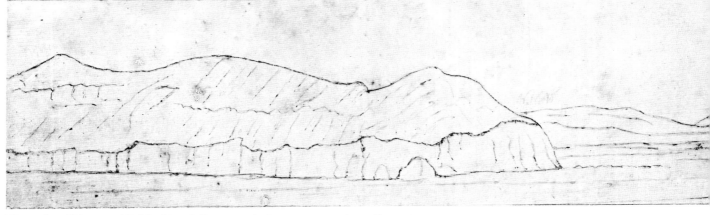

Plate 6. *"Young Nick's Head & part of the entrance into Poverty Bay, New Zealand."* Probably drawn by Sydney Parkinson.

spying glass take a peep at our situation; Dr Solander setts at the Cabbin table describing, myself at my Bureaux Journalizing, between us hangs a large bunch of sea weed, upon the table lays the wood and barnacles; they would see that notwithstanding our different occupations our lips move very often, and without being conjurors might guess that we were talking about what we should see upon the land which there is now no doubt we shall see very soon.'

It was at 2 p.m. on Saturday, 7 October 1769 (nautical time*) or 6 October 1769 (civil time), that land was seen from the masthead by the sharp eyes of Nicholas Young, the surgeon's boy. Although he was only 12 years old he received his reward and in the evening celebrations were held

to mark the occasion. Cook had followed faithfully the Admiralty's instructions and the landfall was made at an observed latitude of 38° 57′ south.

In clear weather Cook worked the *Endeavour* in towards the shore, tacking backwards and forwards in a light northerly breeze. As the ship approached land the artists were busy, and others speculated on the nature of the country or watched the inhabitants through their glasses. Cook thus described the

*Cook used 'nautical time' for the entries in his journal when he was at sea—thus his date was altered at noon. While he was in harbour he generally used 'civil time' with a change of date at midnight. When re-writing his journal he often translated nautical into civil time. To avoid this confusion and, as the day is now universally reckoned to start at midnight, we have converted Cook's time to civil time, as was used by Joseph Banks.

Plate 7 (left). *Aerial view of Young Nick's Head. Beyond, the Waipaoa River reaches the sea several miles to the south of its entry in 1769.*

Plate 8 (right). *Te Oneroa. One of five sketches forming a panorama of Poverty Bay drawn from the* Endeavour *as she lay at anchor. In his panorama the artist, probably Herman Spöring, showed the smoke of thirteen large fires. Here the smoke from one fire is seen behind Kaiti Hill, near the mouth of the Turanganui River, where Gisborne now stands.*

scene—'The land on the Sea-Coast is high with white steep clifts and back inland are very high mountains, the face of the Country is of a hilly surface and appears to be cloathed with wood and Verdure.' Banks was also impressed by the size of the country and the height of the mountains, for he wrote—'Much difference of opinion and many conjectures about Islands, rivers, inlets &c, but all hands seem to agree that this is certainly the Continent we are in search of.'

At midday on Monday, 8 October 1769, the *Endeavour* lay off Young Nick's Head in fine weather (plates 6 and 7). Cook decided to enter the bay and shaped his course for the mouth of a small river where he hoped to obtain fresh water. Along the north-east and south-west shores were steep white cliffs but the land at the head of the bay was low-lying and sandy. As the *Endeavour* glided slowly along several canoes were seen moving quietly across the bay, a curious high palisade was noticed on top of the northern headland and some low houses were observed near the beach where clusters of people were collecting to watch with interest the arrival of the mysterious visitors. By 4 p.m. the ship had reached a point 1½ miles from the shore and the anchor was dropped in 10 fathoms of water, opposite the mouth of the river which entered the north-east side of the bay (plate 8). Banks wrote, 'Here we saw many great smoaks, some near the beach others between the hills, some very far within the land, which we looked upon as great indications of a populous countrey.'

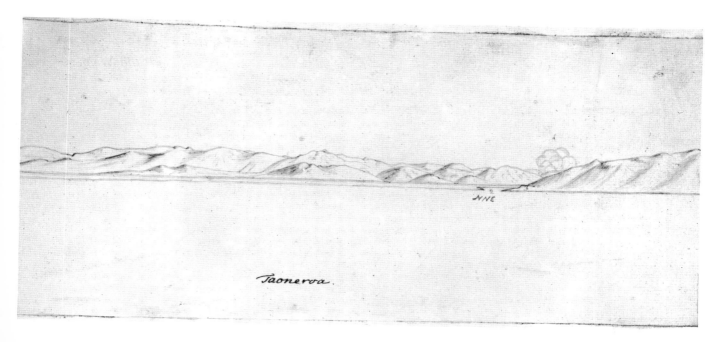

NNE

Taoneroa.

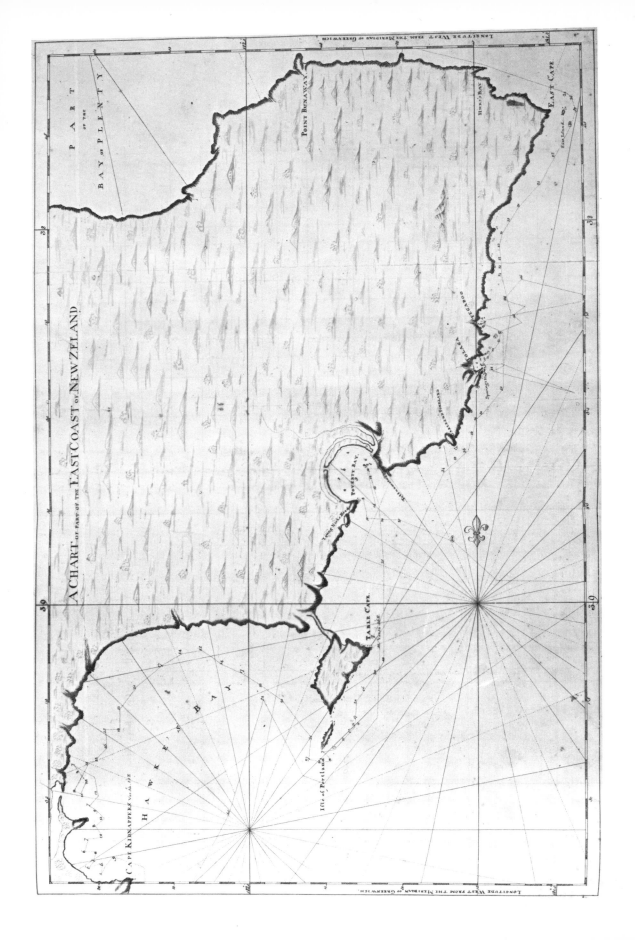

2 The Landing

*You are likewise to observe the Genius, Temper,
Disposition and Number of the Natives, if there be
any, and endeavour by all proper means to cultivate a
Friendship and Alliance with them*

Admiralty Instructions

Since leaving Tahiti the *Endeavour* had been at sea for 2 months and supplies of drinking water, wood and fresh food were running low. In addition, some of the crew were sick, perhaps showing incipient signs of 'sea scurvy'. Moreover, the indications of a thickly populated country made it all the more necessary that friendly relations with the natives should be established as soon as possible to assist in replenishing the needs of the vessel.

Cook immediately prepared to go ashore. Doubtless remembering Tasman's account of the hostile reception by the Maoris which had prevented his landing in 1642, he had the swivel guns brought up on deck and mounted in the boats (plate 10). The yawl and the pinnace were lowered and Cook, Banks and Solander, together with a party of marines, made for the beach. They landed in a gut in the papa shelf—later known as the Boat Harbour—a little to the east of the mouth of the Turanganui River, and separated from it by a narrow ledge of rocks (plate 11). The natives, however, seemed to have withdrawn to the opposite bank of the river and, as it was too deep to ford, Cook and the scientists crossed in the yawl and landed just above the junction of the Waikanae Stream, leaving four boys to look after

Plate 9 (left). *A chart of part of the east coast of the North Island of New Zealand, showing the track of the* Endeavour. *Drawn by J. Cook.*

Plate 10 (right). *The En-deavour's boats. At the top left is the pinnace, below it the long boat and, at the bottom right, the yawl. Sketches by Sydney Parkinson.*

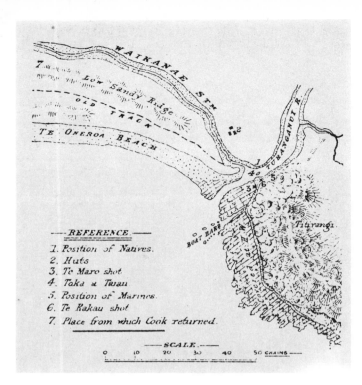

Plate 11. *Sketch of Cook's landing place.*
After Archdeacon W. L. Williams, 1888.

— REFERENCE —
1. Position of Natives.
2. Huts.
3. Te Maro shot.
4. Toka & Tarau
5. Position of Marines.
6. Te Rakau shot.
7. Place from which Cook returned.

the boat, while the marines in the pinnace kept guard at the mouth of the river.

Cook and the scientists, accompanied by Dr Monkhouse, walked about 300 yards to a group of huts where they had hoped to meet the natives, but found them deserted. 'These huts', wrote Monkhouse, 'were very low, the walling of reeds, and thatched with a kind of rush and course grass. Part of these huts were of the wigwam construction consisting of a roof supported by a pole on one side, and a small or narrow piece of walling on the other; but there was one tolerable house about eight yards by six, the end wall of which, where the door and a window to answer the double purpose of admitting light and giving passage to the smoak were situated, was placed about two feet within the roof and side walls; the door way was exceedingly low and narrow so that it was necessary to crawl in'. Lying nearby were some old fishing nets and, set upon a burnt and blackened tree stump, was a piece of white pumice crudely carved into the shape of a human figure. As this object was thought to have a religious significance it was carefully replaced and ornamented with beads and nails. Suddenly, several musket shots rang out and, in some alarm, the party hastily returned to the river bank.

Here they found that the boys in the yawl had landed on the opposite bank of the river to amuse themselves but had soon been attacked by four natives who had concealed themselves in a patch of bush which then grew along the foot of Kaiti Hill just above high-water mark behind the landing place. On seeing this attack the coxswain of the pinnace covering the landing fired a musket shot over their heads. This caused the natives to stop but, as they took no notice of a second warning shot, the coxswain levelled his gun at the leader, killing him on the spot just as he reached the yawl. After recovering from their surprise the three remaining Maoris carried off the body of their companion about 100 yards before leaving it, and slowly withdrew. This was the unhappy scene which greeted Cook, Banks and Solander on their return to the river. They crossed over and hurried to the place where the body had been left.

The Maori, later identified as Te Maro, who belonged to the Ngationeone hapu of the Teitanga-a-Hauiti tribe, had been shot through the heart. He was a short, thickset man about 5 feet 3 inches in height, with the right cheek and nose tattooed in a spiral fashion and with three arched tattoo lines over his left forehead—the rest of his face was unmarked. He had a short beard and his coarse black hair was tied in a knot at the top of his head. His complexion was brown and he wore a cloak quite unlike anything seen in Tahiti, which was accurately described by the observant Monkhouse who made a careful examination of the details of its structure (plate 12). 'He had on him a dress of singular manufacture—the warp consisted of small parcels of the fibres of some plant not twined or formed into thread, but the cross threads were properly twined, and run in parcels of two or three together with an interval of about four lines* between each parcel; a strong selvage thread run along each side but the ends appeared as if cut out of a web of the manufacture—this cloth might be about four feet by three—descended from his neck to the buttocks, compleatly covering the back—its upper corners were turned back and tied—from the upper angle of this reflected part on each side went a string which tied across the neck before—the lower part on each side was brought across the hips and secured with a kind of sedge leaf passed round the loins.'

*A line measured the twelfth part of an inch.

12

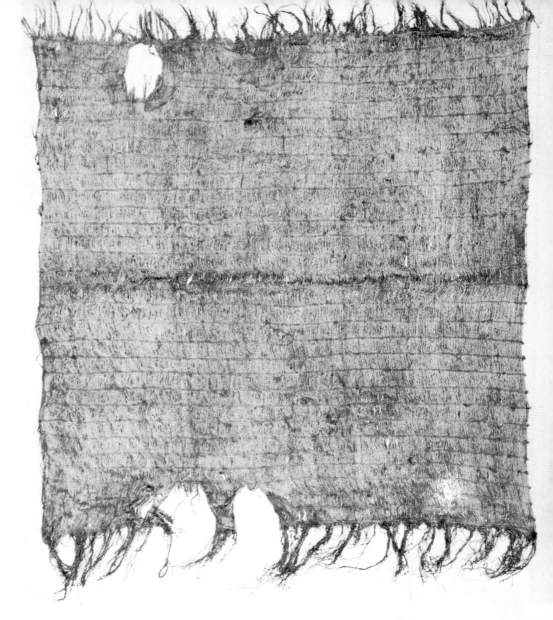

Plates 12a and 12b. *This cloak was collected by Banks and is now in the Alströmer Collection of the Ethnographical Museum of Sweden in Stockholm. Its structure is the same as that described by Monkhouse.*

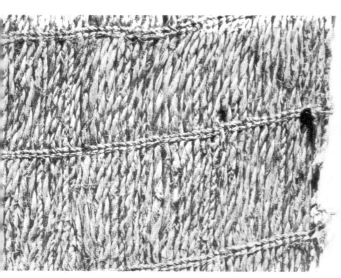

Leaving some nails and beads upon the body, the party then embarked and reached the ship about 6 p.m. Banks wrote in his journal, 'Soon after we came on board we heard the people ashore very distinctly talking very loud no doubt, as they were not less than two miles distant from us, consulting probably what is to be done tomorrow'. We can imagine that the same question was debated in the great cabin on that evening of the first landing on Monday, 8 October 1769.

When James Cook left England he carried with him not only detailed instructions from the Admiralty for the conduct of the voyage but, in addition, 'hints' offered by James Douglas, Earl of Morton and president of the Royal Society, as

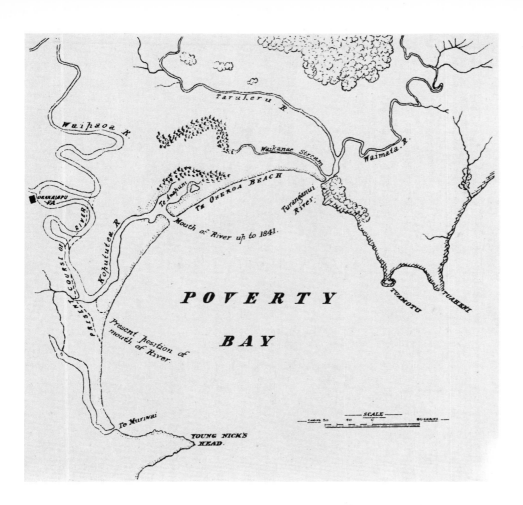

Plate 13. *Sketch of Poverty Bay to show the conditions prevailing at the time of the Endeavour's visit includes the information collected by W. L. Williams in 1888.*

to how best to achieve the scientific aims of the expedition. Included was enlightened and humane advice on the subject of making friends with the native peoples who might be encountered on the voyage. It was necessary to use the utmost patience and forbearance and, in order to avoid bloodshed, to restrain the wanton use of firearms by the sailors. It should be remembered that the native people had the right to occupy any part of their country and it was natural and just that they should attempt to repel intruders. There were many ways to convince them of the superiority of European arms without killing them, for example, by shooting some bird or animal nearby, by killing a bird on the wing or by knocking down some conspicuous object with a great shot. Presents might be left on the shore, but if during an inevitable skirmish some natives were slain, the survivors should be made to realise that it was only done in self-defence, and they should be treated 'with distinguished humanity'.

In the early stages of the voyage no difficulty

had arisen in establishing friendly relations with the natives in Tierra del Fuego for they had already learned of the superiority of European weapons. In Tahiti also, the natives were well enough acquainted with visitors from Europe and their needs. Now, however, Cook was meeting for the first time a proud and warlike people as yet ignorant of the devastating power of firearms, but willing to defend their country bravely with what weapons they possessed.

Effective in theory, Lord Morton's hints proved to be difficult to apply in practice. But, unlike Tasman, Cook was determined to continue his efforts, for on their success depended the outcome of the voyage.

Next morning it was planned to try once more to make friends with the natives who could be seen moving about on the beach. Cook decided to take a strong party of marines and to use the long boat in addition to the pinnace and the yawl. A high surf prevented entry to the river or a landing on the western bank, where the Maoris were beginning to collect. Cook, mistaking this for a sign of fear ordered the yawl to the boat harbour where he, Banks and Solander landed. He then walked alone up the east bank of the Turanganui River and called across to the natives in the Tahitian language, which they seemed to understand. The Maoris, however, drew together and began a war dance 'by no means unpleasing to Spectators at a distance' and described by Lieutenant John Gore thus, 'About an hundred of the Natives all Arm'd came down on the opposite side of the Salt River, drew themselves up in lines. Then with a Regular Jump from Left to Right and the Reverse, They brandish'd Their Weapons, distort'd their Mouths, Lolling out their Tongues and Turn'd up the Whites of their Eyes Accompanied with a strong hoarse song, Calculated in my opinion to Chear Each Other and Intimidate their Enemies, and may be call'd perhaps with propiety A Dancing War Song. It lasted 3 or 4 minutes'. There could be no doubt of the hostile intentions of the natives, and indeed, Maori tradition identifies these warriors as members of the Rongowhakaata tribe from the Orakaiapu pa on the Waipaoa River, who had seen the *Endeavour* arrive the previous day. They thought it was a floating island and were determined to capture it.

The splash of a musket ball, fired wide, temporarily subdued this warlike demonstration while Cook withdrew his party to the landing place and ordered the marines ashore. Carrying a flag they marched to a small flat area some 50 yards from the river where they were drawn up in support. Viewing these manoeuvres from the ship, Parkinson concluded erroneously that Cook was taking possession of the country. Dr Monkhouse, Mr Green the astronomer, and Tupaia were added to the advance party which again walked towards the natives. Tupaia spoke to the Maoris in the Tahitian language, which they readily understood, and explained that the visitors were friends and needed water and provisions for which they would be given iron and beads in exchange. A nail was thrown across the river but it fell short. At last, however, one of the natives swam unarmed to an island, named Te Toka a Taiau, in the middle of the river, but would come no further. Cook then handed his musket to an attendant and waded over to the island to meet the Maori. After saluting each other by touching noses Cook gave him some trinkets. This prompted two more natives to swim over to the island but they brought with them their weapons 'artfully concealed' below the water. Cook's anxiety to make friends had thus placed him in a position of extreme danger, outnumbered, unarmed and separated from his companions, but fortunately, after distributing all the presents he had with him, he was able to return safely to the shore. The ice was broken and soon all the Maoris crossed the river, but they brought their arms with them. Spike nails and beads meant little to these warriors, who were willing only to exchange weapons.

Eventually, growing bolder, one of the natives snatched Mr Green's sword and, waving it round his head in triumph, retreated towards the river. Such effrontery demanded instant action and Cook ordered Banks to fire. A charge of small shot from 15 yards struck the man between the shoulders but he continued to withdraw. Dr Monkhouse, whose musket was loaded with ball, was then ordered to fire and the man dropped. Several of his companions rushed back and tore his green-stone mere from his wrist but Dr Monkhouse was able to retrieve the stolen sword. Cook, Green and Tupaia fired charges of small shot at these natives who, though slightly wounded, retreated past the rock to their fellows on the western bank. The fallen Maori, whose name was Te Rakau, was mortally wounded but he was able to speak to Tupaia before he died.

As nothing more could be done with these hostile natives and because the water in the river was salt, Cook decided to embark his forces and search elsewhere for a supply of fresh water and a more promising place to land. He also intended if possible 'to surprise some of the natives and to take them on board and by good treatment and presents endeavour to gain their friendship.'

In the afternoon, therefore, the three boats proceeded towards the south side of the bay but a landing proved impossible for 'the sea broke most prodigiously' all along the low sandy beach. Then two canoes were seen coming in from the sea and making for the entrance of the Kopututea River, which at that time entered the centre of the bay well to the north of its present outlet. Cook decided to capture the leading canoe which, with seven people on board, had sailed unsuspectingly into the middle of his group of boats. Tupaia called to the natives to come alongside and told them that they would not be hurt; but, instead, they lowered the sail and began to paddle off at high speed. A musket shot was fired over their

Plate 14. *Aerial view of the city of Gisborne in 1969. The structure near the confluence of the Waikanae Stream with the Turanganui River marks the site of the rock Te Toka a Taiau. The landing place is just beyond the longer breakwater.*

heads and the canoe stopped, but, as soon as Cook's pinnace came up they attacked so vigorously, with stones, paddles and even a bundle of fish, that fire was opened and four of them were killed. The three remaining jumped overboard. Two boys were captured quite easily, but the other, a young man of twenty, nearly eluded his captors by swimming and diving with great agility. Surprised at being alive and by the unexpected kindness of those in the boats who gave them clothes and fed them on salt pork and biscuits, the youths soon seemed to recover their good spirits. After a tiring row against the wind the boats reached the *Endeavour*

about 5 p.m.

The names of the young Maoris captured were Te Haurangi and Ikirangi, who were brothers, and Marukauiti. They talked readily with Tupaia and asked and answered questions. They entertained their captors with a dance and a song and, at dinner, they insisted on tasting everything. They were particularly fond of salt pork and bread and their appetites were impressive. Sydney Parkinson wrote, 'These men, while on board, ate an immoderate quantity of everything that was set before them, taking pieces at one time into their mouths six times larger than we did, and drank a quart of wine and water at one draught.'

But it had been a disastrous day. In the rough notes he made at the time Cook wrote, 'I can by no means justify my conduct in attacking and killing the people in this boat who had given me no just provication and was wholly igernorant of my design and had I had the least thought of their making any resistance I would not so much as looked at them, but when we was once a long side of them we must either have stud to be knockd on the head or else retire and let them gone off in triumph and this last they would of Course have attributed to their own bravery and our timorousness'. Banks was no less distressed by the turn of events, 'Thus ended the most disagreable day My life has yet seen, black be the mark for it and heaven send that such may never return to embitter future reflection'.

The weather continued fine and early next morning, Wednesday, 10 October 1769, a boat was sent ashore with a party to cut wood under the protection of a force of marines. Soon after, Cook, Banks, Solander and Tupaia followed, taking with them the three boys, for they were anxious to see what effect their kindly treatment of them would have on the other Maoris. Once again the landing was made at the boat harbour. The boys were unwilling to land in hostile territory and hid in the bushes, claiming that they were afraid of being killed and eaten by their enemies.

Cook and the scientists crossed the Turanganui River and walked along the banks of the Waikanae Stream shooting ducks which were numerous there, while Banks and Solander collected plants. A sergeant and four marines accompanied them and kept a lookout from a ridge of sandhills running parallel with the stream. When the party had gone about a mile a large body of about 200 natives was seen approaching. Cook decided to retreat and they all moved quickly along the Te Oneroa beach to the Turanganui River and were ferried across to the eastern shore. The Maoris were gathering on the opposite side of the river when the boys recognised them as friends. At last, the uncle of Marukauiti, the youngest of the boys, was induced to cross the river. He came carrying a green stick as an emblem of peace and was given presents by everyone including the boys. Later he chose to go back to his friends but the boys preferred to return to the Endeavour.

Realising that nothing more could be achieved in this place without further bloodshed, Cook

wisely decided to sail next day. The boys were therefore taken ashore again and left there against their wishes. Those on board were relieved to see them rafted across the river to join their friends by whom they were soon surrounded. They spent about an hour on the river bank, no doubt recounting their experiences and, just before dark came down to the shore and waved three times to the ship, before moving off with the others towards their village.

The Maoris had lived in this district for many years. They knew it as Turanga-nui-Kiwa, 'the great abiding place of Kiwa', who was one of the chiefs of the *Takitimu* canoe, which had made its landfall at the Mahia Peninsula just to the south of this bay. But great changes were soon to come and now the city of Gisborne stands at the mouth of the Turanganui River to serve the needs of the community which farms the rich alluvial plains nearby. Fortunately, the places described by Cook and his officers could still be recognised more than 100 years after his visit, which allowed Archdeacon W. L. Williams to construct a map in 1888 to record their position (plate 13). Since then the construction of harbour facilities in the Turanganui River has obscured some of these landmarks, but many of the geographical features may still be identified in an aerial photograph (plate 14). The ledge of rocks extending out from the base of Kaiti Hill near the eastern breakwater still marks Cook's landing place, the wharf and buildings on the western breakwater opposite the mouth of the Waikanae Stream indicate the position of the rock known as Te Toka a Taiau, the Waikanae Stream where Cook shot his ducks is clearly seen while the surf still rolls in along Te Oneroa or Waikanae Beach.

But to those on board the *Endeavour* this place had yielded nothing but worry and frustration. And so, at 6 a.m., on 11 October 1769, Cook ordered the anchor to be weighed and the ship stood out to sea. Attempts to make friends with the warlike inhabitants of New Zealand seemed to have been a dismal failure. Neither fresh water nor food had been obtained. The scientists had been able to collect fewer than 40 botanical specimens and their artists had not even been able to leave the ship. As an anchorage too, the bay had 'nothing to recommend it', and Cook, who had first called it Endeavour Bay, in his disappointment renamed it Poverty Bay, 'because it afforded us no one thing we wanted'.

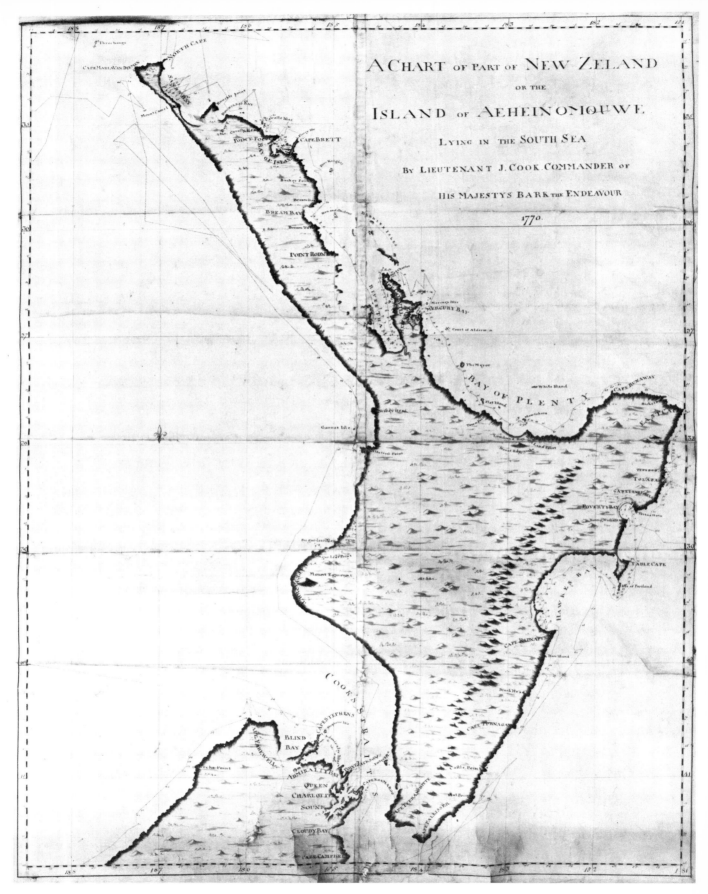

A CHART of PART of NEW ZELAND

OR THE

ISLAND of AEHEINOMOUWE

LYING IN THE SOUTH SEA

BY LIEUTENANT J. COOK COMMANDER of

HIS MAJESTYS BARK THE ENDEAVOUR

1770

3 Te Ika a Maui

This he calld Aeheino mouwe a name many others
before had call'd it by

James Cook

After the unsuccessful interlude in Poverty Bay Cook decided to sail south to the latitude of 40° S in accordance with the Admiralty's instructions. If nothing more encouraging was found he planned to turn north to explore and chart the coastline and, if possible, replenish his supplies.

Moving slowly along the shore with a following northerly breeze the *Endeavour* was soon approached by 7 canoes containing some 50 men. While Tupaia was trying to persuade them to come nearer another canoe appeared from the direction of Poverty Bay and made directly for the ship. The four occupants came aboard without fear or hesitation. Banks, who recognised one of the men, asked what had become of the young boys who had been put on shore the previous day and was relieved to learn that they were unhurt and at home. The Maoris also let it be known that it was the boys'

account of their kind treatment on board the *Endeavour* which had prompted their own visit to the ship. Soon after, the men from the other canoes climbed aboard and began to trade their belongings with great enthusiasm. One group of Maoris, after having bartered their clothes and paddles, offered to sell their canoe. This friendly visit lasted some 2 hours until the evening, when the Maoris set off for the shore, leaving three of their number behind.

This encouraging incident must have seemed to confirm Lord Morton's opinion that 'the most savage and brutal Nations are more easily gained by mild, than by rough treatment'. It did, in fact, mark the turning point in the visitors' relations with the Maori people.

Joseph Banks, fearing further bloodshed amongst other tribes which had not experienced the power

Plate 15 (left). *A chart of the North Island of New Zealand by Lieutenant J. Cook.*

Plate 16 (above). *A large war canoe as seen from the* Endeavour, *after a drawing by Sydney Parkinson.*

of the musket or the benefits of trade, wished to accept the invitation of the Maoris to go ashore in this friendly atmosphere, but Cook was not to be diverted from his plan. As the *Endeavour* sailed slowly south past the Mahia Peninsula and along the shores of a wide bay which Cook named Hawke's Bay, after Sir Edward Hawke, First Lord of the Admiralty, it was visited by a large number of canoes. Some were fishing canoes whose occupants were willing to trade their catch. Others were large war canoes (plate 16) filled with hostile warriors shouting, 'Haere mai, haere mai, haere ki uta hei patu-patu ake,★ whose attentions it was necessary to divert with shots, fired wide, from the 4-pound cannon.

Manned by a double row of tattooed warriors, their paddles flashing in perfect time with the canoe chants of a leader standing amidship and brandishing a greenstone club or mere, the speeding war canoe, with its feather streamers floating out behind, must have been an awesome sight. 'I have seen 15 paddles of a side in one of their Canoes move with immensely quick strokes and at the same time as much Justness as if the movers were animated by one Soul', wrote Banks, 'not the

★'Come here, come here, come on shore to be patu-patued!'

fraction of a second could be observd between the dipping and raising any two of them, the Canoe all the While moving with incredible swiftness'.

The war dance was equally calculated to impress the enemy. Sydney Parkinson illustrated the weapons and menacing gestures and William Monkhouse described the performance thus, 'They treated us with a kind of *Heiva* or war dance performed by striking their paddles upon the gunwell, laid across for that Purpose, beating time in exact regularity to the parts of a Song which they chanted in a very martial tone. A Man in the headmost Canoe at the same time, standing erect, Shouldered, poised, & brandished his paddle with the true spirit of a Veteran. In some of his gesticulations great savageness was expressed—in bending forward, throwing his Arms behind him, elevating his head, staring wildly upwards, and thrusting his tongue forward, he exhibited a figure very like that expressed in the heads of their Canoes. He did this at the close of the song, pronouncing the last sentence with a strong hoarse expiration— the rest followed his example in the last manoeuvre'.

The war canoe itself was an impressive craft capable of carrying up to 100 men and, with its sail set, able to travel fast before the wind over

Plate 17. *"View of Cape Kidnappers from the S.E." By Herman Spöring.*

20

Plate 18. *Gannets now nest in serried rows on the top of the headland.*

long distances. The size of the great totara and kauri trees growing in the New Zealand bush enabled the Maoris to construct canoes so large and stable that double canoes of the Polynesian type were found to be unnecessary and gradually disappeared from the scene. Nevertheless, for long ocean voyages, two canoes were often lashed together to increase stability. Measuring 5 feet in width, $3\frac{1}{2}$ feet in depth and 70 or more feet in length, the canoe was made in three parts with the bow and stern sections attached to the longer central section by mortice and tenon joins. Cook measured gunwale strakes made of planks 63 feet long, 12 inches broad and $1\frac{1}{4}$ inches thick, well fitted and lashed to the hull. But it was in the intricate carving of the bow and stern pieces that the Maori craftsman was able to display his great artistry and skill, well shown in the detailed drawing of Herman Spöring (plate 33).

By Sunday morning, 15 October 1769, the *Endeavour* had reached the southern point of Hawke Bay and was surrounded by canoes trading fish for Tahitian tapa cloth of which the Maoris were extremely fond. A canoe containing 22 armed men then arrived, amongst whom was one wearing a black skin cloak which Cook was anxious to obtain in order to judge 'what sort of Animal the first owner was'. He offered a piece of red baize in exchange and a bargain was struck. On receiving the cloth, however, the man refused to part with his cloak. While some of the officers were planning a reprisal by throwing a running bowline over the head of the canoe, the Maoris grabbed Taiata, Tupaia's Tahitian boy, who was handing up the bartered goods, hauled him into one of the canoes and made off. The marines were ordered to fire. Two or three of the kidnappers were killed and, in the confusion, Taiata jumped overboard and was rescued. To mark the site of this daring attempt Cook named the nearby point of land Cape Kidnappers and Spöring sketched it with his usual accuracy (plate 17).

This prominent landmark was known to the Maoris, appropriately enough, as Mataupo Maui—

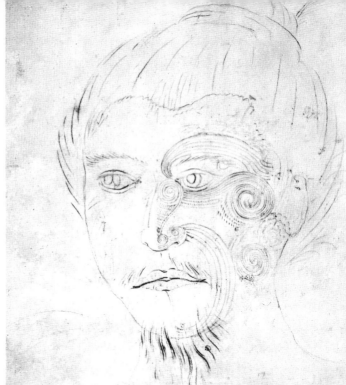

Plate 19 (left). *"Portrait of a New Zeland Man." A wash drawing which Parkinson made from his preliminary sketch.*

Plate 20 (above). *"Sketch of a New Zeland Man." By Sydney Parkinson.*

the fish hook of Maui. It is remarkable today as the only nesting place of the gannet on the mainland of New Zealand (plate 18). Gannets do not appear to have started to nest here until about 100 years after Cook's visit but, by 1880, 50 birds were counted. Since then the numbers have increased greatly until now many thousands of pairs of these beautiful birds, nesting in orderly rows, have transformed Cape Kidnappers into one of the most exciting natural spectacles in the country.

Next day the *Endeavour* reached the latitude of 40° 34′ S and, as there was no sign of a harbour and no likelihood of obtaining water, Cook decided to waste no more time. At Cape Turnagain he headed the bow of the *Endeavour* to the north.

While passing the Mahia Peninsula the ship was boarded by two Maori chiefs who insisted on staying the night, together with their three slaves. They seemed interested in all they saw and were grateful for the presents which they were given. Those in the *Endeavour* were equally interested in

their visitors and continued to make the most of their unique opportunity to learn as much as possible about the Maori people, as yet uninfluenced by the outside world. The clothing, ornaments, weapons and language were studied and the tattooing, being unlike that seen previously in Tahiti, received particular attention. Sydney Parkinson drew several portraits of Maori chiefs showing different patterns of tattooing (plates 19 and 20), while Dr Monkhouse examined the facial carving with a professional eye. 'A well finished face has no part untouched but the upper part of the forehead: and in this state they look as black as any Negroe whatever. All below the forehead is done in Spirals—over each eye are broad arches. . . . I observed one Man to day to have arches over his eyebrows about two lines broad and filled with variously curved small lines in carving as it were— as if a plate for example had been graved with numberless little flourishes confined within two arched lines, and empressed upon the part; and each little curve thus mark'd out, not by a simple line or superficial black mark but really indented in the Skin'.

The deeply incised tattooing of the Maori artists differed from the smooth punctured patterns found elsewhere in Polynesia. In addition to the traditional comb-like teeth of the bone blades used for tattooing in other islands of the Pacific, the Maori craftsmen employed a bone blade ground to a smooth cutting edge, similar to the tools developed for their intricate carving in wood. Tapping such an instrument with his mallet the tattooer cut through the skin by the continued application of the narrow cutting blade. The pigment was derived from soot made by burning the resinous heartwood of the white pine or kauri tree. The sufferings of the subject may be inferred from the beautifully carved wooden funnels which were used to feed him until the pain and swelling of his face subsided.

Continuing to the north past the entrance to Poverty Bay Cook brought the *Endeavour* to an anchorage in a shallow bay some 20 miles north of Gable End Foreland. He named this bay Tegadoo, possibly his interpretation of Te ngaru—the breakers—which he may have elicited from the Maoris in error as the name of the bay, which, in fact, they knew as Anaura.

The ship was soon surrounded by canoes and Cook, seeing two old men whose dress suggested

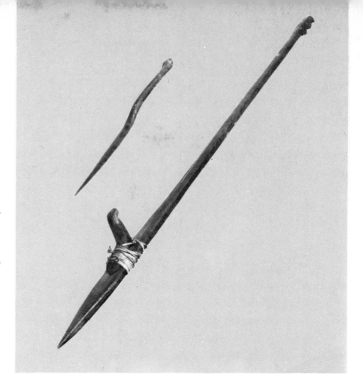

Plate 21. *Tools used by the Maoris for cultivating their root crops. On the left is the paddle shaped weeder known variously as the pinaki, ketu, or wauwau. To the right is their chief agricultural tool or ko which was used for planting kumara and digging fern root or aruhe.*

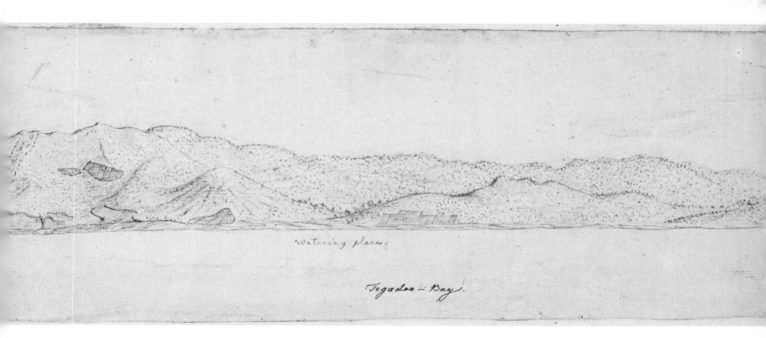

Plate 22. *"Tegadoo Bay" by Herman Spöring shows the position of the watering place at Anaura and the Maori vegetable gardens cut out of the bush. Sketched from the* Endeavour *at anchor in the bay.*

that they were chiefs, invited them on board and presented to each four yards of linen and a spike nail. Tupaia explained to them the reason for the visit and its peaceful nature. Later in the afternoon a party reached the shore and filled some casks with fresh water from a small stream, though great difficulty was experienced in getting them back to the ship through the tremendous surf. However, the natives were friendly and Cook decided to stay another day to allow the scientists 'to collect a little of the produce of the Country'.

Accordingly next day, on 21 October 1769, Banks and Solander landed safely and spent the day collecting plants and 'shooting some most beautiful birds'. They visited several of the houses of the Maoris and were most impressed by their well cultivated gardens. 'In them', Banks wrote, 'were planted sweet potatoes, cocos [yams] and some one of the cucumber kind [taro], as we judgd from the seed leaves which just appeard above ground; the first of these were planted in small hills, some rangd in rows other in quincunx* all laid by a line most regularly, the Cocos were planted on flat land and not yet appeard above ground, the Cucumbers were set in small hollows or dishes much as we do

*An arrangement of five plants, so as to occupy each corner and the centre of a square.

in England. These plantations were from 1 or 2 to 8 or 10 acres each, in the bay might be 150 or 200 acres in cultivation tho we did not see 100 people in all. Each distinct patch was fencd in generaly with reeds placd close one by another so that scarce a mouse could creep through'.

Dr William Monkhouse, a trained observer, fortunately did not confine his attention to medicine. He moved freely around the village making detailed observations about the people, their houses and customs. He, too, was surprised to find such well tended gardens. 'The ground is compleatly cleared of all weeds—the mold broke with as much care as that of our best gardens'. He described the two kinds of digging tools used to cultivate the ground, 'one was short and pointed, about three inches broad and thirty inches long [pinaki]—the other, formed much in the same way, was not broader but about Six feet long [ko]' (plate 21).

The exact size and position of these gardens are known from the detailed and accurate work of Herman Spöring, whose artistic 'views' and sketches combine a rare charm with photographic accuracy. With the death of Alexander Buchan during an epileptic seizure in Tahiti the expedition lost its official landscape and figure painter. This disaster was mitigated by the efforts of Spöring who was able to assist Sydney Parkinson to cope with the tremendous load of illustration which fell to his

Plate 23. *Anaura Bay from a position similar to that from which Spöring made his sketch* (Plate 22).

lot. Herman Spöring, appointed as Banks's secretary, was also a draughtsman of great ability. Whenever the *Endeavour* anchored he seems to have made a pencil sketch of the surrounding country from the deck of the ship. Some of these 'views' are panoramas made up from as many as seven individual drawings. As the *Endeavour* moved along the coast he made other sketches with great accuracy of line and truth of proportion. From these drawings, all carefully annotated with compass bearings, the position of the *Endeavour* may be readily deduced. Moreover, they permit rapid recognition of the places visited and make obvious the changes which have occurred in the past 200 years. These sketches have been preserved in the Banks Collection of the British Museum and it is with great pleasure that we reproduce some of them here for the first time.

Plate 22 is one of five drawings of Tegadoo Bay (Anaura) which cover the whole sweep of the coast from Marau Point to Mawhai Point. Drawn from the *Endeavour* anchored in the bay, it shows the watering place as the more southerly of the two small streams which here enter the sea. The gardens which so impressed Banks and Monkhouse are clearly shown cut out of the dense bush which then clothed the hills. Although the trees have long since been felled no difficulty is experienced in identifying the position of the cultivations, and it is interesting to note that crops are still being harvested today from the site of one of the old Maori gardens which Spöring showed at the base of the hill just to the north of the watering place (plate 23).

Before he returned to the *Endeavour* Dr Monkhouse was entertained by the Maoris to a meal which he vividly described thus: 'In contemplating the people as they were moving about me I observed two old Men, who appeared as chiefs, going to dinner—glad of the opportunity I immediately introduced myself by means of my beads &c. and was recieved very cordially. They were seated upon the grass—a young man had made a fire a short distance from them—he had a quantity of roots each about nine inches long, a flat large pebble, and a wooden mallet by him—some of these roots were roasting upon the fire he attended and turned them till they were thoroughly heated—he then beat them, one at a time, doubled and beat them again, and when fully softned he threw them to the Chiefs, who now were employed eating a lobster that had been dressed but was now cold. A woman had brought them this lobster, and afterwards brought them another, from a contiguous hut. They eat the lobster and roots just as we would lobster and bread. I partook with them of the repast—but we had nothing to drink—I pulled out my brandy bottle and took some to invite them—they tasted with me, and did not seem much to dislike it which surprized me exceedingly. Several other people of both sexes were sitting by us but nobody eat besides these two chiefs'.

These lobsters, which were caught by the women amongst the rocks at low tide, were greatly esteemed by the visitors. Parkinson found that each one weighed about 11 pounds and Banks pronounced them as 'certainly the largest and best I have ever eat.' An unknown artist, amongst the crew, depicted a Maori bartering one of these large crayfish with one of the *Endeavour's* company for a piece of tapa cloth (plate 24).

Banks and Solander, anxious to get their specimens on board before dark, were paddled out to the ship in one of the canoes—but not before they had overturned it in the surf and got well soused. Parkinson's beautiful drawings of some of these plants may still be seen in the Banks Collection of the British Museum (plate 25).

Bad weather forced the *Endeavour* off shore, but on the following day it was learned from some fishermen that water was to be procured in a sheltered bay a little to the south. Cook therefore followed along the coast until he found a shallow bay where he anchored his ship about 1 mile from the southern headland. He thought the natives' name for this bay was Tolaga, but again he was misled, possibly confusing their word turanga—a landing place—given in answer to his query. The Maori name was really Uawa.

Just round the southern headland of this bay Cook found the snug little haven, known to the Maoris as Opoutama, where wood and water could readily be obtained. The entrance from the sea has altered little since Spöring made his sketch (plate 26). The perforated fretwork of the Mitre Rocks and the stratified white cliffs of Pourewa (all of which Cook named Spöring's Islands) are still there to break the force of the ocean swell (plate 27).

This place, now known as Cooks Cove, offered all that the ship required, and, as the natives were friendly and anxious to trade, Cook decided to stay for several days (plate 28). On 25 October 1769, he took several observations of the sun and moon and calculated the longitude to be 180° 47′ west of

Plate 24. *A Maori barters a crayfish for a piece of tapa cloth, by an unknown artist on the* Endeavour.

Plate 25. *Tree fuchsia collected at "Tegadu" (Anaura Bay). On the back of his unfinished drawing Sydney Parkinson wrote in pencil, "The calyx deep Crimson on the inside as are also the filaments & stile the top of which is yellow. The petals dark purple the outside of the calyx paler & ting'd wt green anthera yellow ting'd wt red the upper part of the leaves dark grass green the under part white wt a cast of green & vein'd wt green the capsula green the stalk gray green". From this drawing and these instructions James Miller made this painting in 1775.*

Sydney Parkinson died at the age of 26 years before the Endeavour *returned to England. His sketches were used by Banks's botanical draughtsmen—F. P. Nodder, J. F. Miller, James Miller, and James Clevely—in the preparation of illustrations for an account of the voyage, which was never published. Parkinson himself did not have time to complete many of his numerous sketches, but Plates 72 and 73 are beautiful examples of his finished work.*

Plate 26 (at top). *Looking south from the* Endeavour *anchored in Tolaga Bay. This sketch by Herman Spöring shows the smoke from the forge at the entrance to the watering place on the right, and the channel separating ''Spöring's Islands'' from the shore.*

Plate 27 (centre). *The approaches to Cooks Cove today.*

Plate 28 (right). *Cook's map of Tolaga Bay, 1769.*

A PLAN of TOLAGA BAY
in
NEW ZELAND
Latitude 38.22 S.
A Sale of One Mile

Plate 29 (above). *"Tolaga Bay". Sydney Parkinson made this sketch from a position near the mouth of the Turanui Stream where it enters Cooks Cove.*

Plate 30 (left). *Clianthus puniceus or kaka beak. This shrub used to grow naturally on the cliffs around Tolaga Bay and was cultivated by the Maoris for the beauty of its flowers. An unsigned painting made from a drawing by Parkinson.*

Greenwich. He then rowed ashore and spent the rest of the day at the watering place. Sydney Parkinson's drawing provides graphic details of the lively scene (plate 29). At the left, or northern shore, smoke is billowing up from the armourer's forge where the broken tiller braces of the *Endeavour* are being repaired. Nearer at hand, at the mouth of the Turanui stream, a bung is being driven into one more cask while sailors manhandle others through the shallow water towards the waiting boat. Some of the Maoris watch the proceedings with interest, though one of their number stands guard over the canoe drawn up on the beach to the right of the picture. By evening 12 tons of water and three boatloads of wood had been ferried out

Plate 31 (above). *"A View of the Great Natural Arch at Tolaga,"* by J. Cook, 1769.

Plate 32 (right). *The archway in 1969.*

to the *Endeavour* and Cook was well pleased with the day's work.

The naturalists were equally delighted with their first real opportunity to collect botanical specimens (plate 30). In their search for plants Banks and Solander walked across a small ridge about 300 yards from the beach and, following down a stream, came upon an 'extraordinary natural curiosity'. Banks described it thus, 'We on a sudden saw a most noble arch or Cavern through the face of a rock leading directly to the sea, so that through it we had not only a view of the bay and hills on the other side but an opportunity of imagining a ship or any other grand object opposite to it. It was certainly the most magnificent

Plate 33. *The head of a Maori war canoe drawn by Herman Spöring on Pourewa or Spörings Island.*

surprize I have ever met with, so much is pure nature superior to art in these cases.' Doubtless copying Parkinson, Cook drew this archway (plate 31), which has altered little in 200 years (plate 32).

During the next 3 days while the watering and the wooding of the ship were being completed, some culinary experiments were carried out on the local flora. The leaves of the 'Tea Plant', or manuka, were used for tea, a 'Cabbage tree' or nikau palm was cut down for the sake of the cabbage which 'ate well boiled', and Cook, never forgetting the health of his men, lost no opportunity to collect 'Sellery' (*Apium australe*) and 'Scurvy grass' (*Lepidium oleraceum*). He wrote, 'this is found here in great plenty and I have caused it to be boild with Portable Soup and Oatmeal every morning for the Peoples breakfast, and this I design to continue as long as it will last or any is to be got because I look upon it to be very wholesome and a great Antiscorbutick.'

On Pourewa Island, Banks examined a war canoe 68½ feet long and Spöring drew the intricate carving of the head and stern pieces in beautiful detail (plate 33). Banks was also impressed by a larger house, some 30 feet long, in which 'all the side posts were carvd in a masterly stile of their whimsical taste which seems confind to the making of spirals and distorted human faces'.

At some time during the daily visits to the watering place a small well was dug out of the hillside about the middle of the northern shore of the cove, some 30 yards from high-water mark and 20 feet above it. Cut into the soft rock it measured 10 inches in diameter and was about 1 foot deep. It served to collect water which trickled down from an overhanging rock and may have refreshed the iron workers at the forge. Known to the Maoris as Te Wai Keri a Tepaea, and by later visitors as Tupaia's Well or Cook's Well, it remained for more than a century the only visible reminder of Cook's visit to Tolaga Bay.

Cook himself left a less enduring monument. In his rough notes made at the time he recorded that he had 'Left an Inscription,' which was described by the anonymous author of an account of the voyage, published by Becket in 1771, as 'cut on a tree a little to the right of our watering place'.

Sydney Parkinson became quite lyrical about the beauty of this cove. He wrote, 'The country about the bay is agreeable beyond description and, with proper cultivation, might be rendered a kind of second Paradise. The hills are covered with beautiful flowering shrubs, intermingled with a great number of tall and stately palms, which fill the air with a most grateful fragrant perfume.'

Today this pleasing picture is sadly changed, for the bush has been destroyed and the grassy hills are almost bare of trees and shrubs (plate 34). With the disappearance of the forest the Turanui Stream has diminished in size and, in summer, often fails to reach the sea. The water course from the spring, though usually dry now, may still be seen though Tupaia's Well, just below the rocky overhang, can no longer be found. The Hole in the Wall, discovered by Banks, was well known to the

Plate 34. *A modern view of Cooks Cove.*

Maoris who called it Te Kotore o te Whenua. It provided them with a useful route when travelling between the cove and their settlement in Tolaga Bay. Two many-headed cabbage trees now frame the valley and the waters of Tolaga Bay shimmer reflected light through the archway. The nikau palms have gone but a few trees still cling around the entrance, enough to suggest the romantic beauty which so fired the imagination of the early explorers.

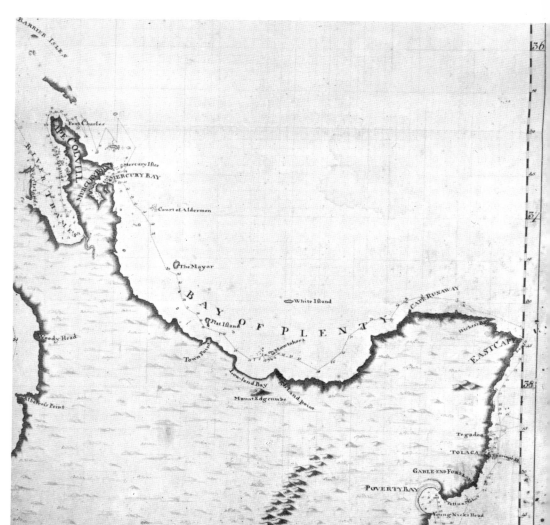

Plate 35. *The* Endeavour's *route from Poverty Bay to Thames. By J. Cook.*

Refreshed after nearly a week at Tolaga Bay, Cook weighed anchor and put to sea at first light on Sunday, 29 October 1769. Once again a course was set for the north and the *Endeavour*, sailing before a brisk breeze, outdistanced all the canoes which put off from the shore. East Cape was rounded (plate 35) and numerous villages and cultivated gardens were seen along the coast. As many as 50 canoes were counted at one time approaching the ship but trading for the most part was orderly and fair. In the evening when the ship was near Motuhora, or Whale Island (plates 36 and 37), the first double canoe seen in New Zealand appeared. Two canoes were lashed together leaving a space of 1 foot between them which was covered with boards. The occupants seemed to talk in a friendly way to Tupaia but, just before dark they threw some stones at the *Endeavour* and made off for the shore near Whakatane. At day-light on the following morning, 2 November 1769, the same canoe appeared. Banks described the encounter, 'A Sailing canoe that had chasd us ever since day break came up with us and provd the same double canoe as pelted us last night which made us prepare for another volley of their ammunition, dangerous to nothing on board but our windows. The event provd as we expected for after having saild with us an hour they threw their stones again; a musquet was fired over them and they dropd astern not I beleive at all frightned by the musquet but content with having shewd their courage by twice insulting us. We now begin to know these people and are much less afraid of any daring attempt from them than we were.' Herman Spöring took the opportunity of making a spirited drawing of the attack (plate 38).

The Maoris showed much ingenuity in manu-facturing the sails of their sea-going canoes which,

The island of Motuhora.

Plate 36 (above). *Sketch by Spöring of the little island of Motuhora or Whale Island, off Whakatane in the Bay of Plenty.*

Plate 37 (right). *Motuhora Island from the south.*

unlike those made elsewhere in Polynesia, were made in one piece, usually being plaited from flax leaves. Only one Maori canoe sail survives as part of 'a collection presented by the Lords of the Admiralty' to the British Museum, and doubtless secured by Cook. The top of the triangular sail and the streamer which flew from it were ornamented with split feathers of the pigeon and hawk while the edges were strengthened by a stout cord. The method of rigging the sail is shown in Spöring's picture. It was permanently fixed along one side to a mast which was stepped in a rope ring and lashed to the side of a thwart and supported by a fore and back stay. The other side, attached to the sprit, was controlled by a rope which was used to fix or manoeuvre the sail. The sail was easily lowered by tying the sprit to the mast, unshipping it and laying the whole along the centre of the thwarts.

Whale Island soon dropped astern and the *Endeavour* passed quickly north between Mayor and The Aldermen Islands and the coast, along which were seen many villages enclosed by palisades and surrounded by ditches. Tupaia believed that these must be places of worship but Cook thought, more realistically, that they were likely to be defensive strongholds.

The transit of the planet Mercury across the sun was due to occur on 9 November 1769, and Cook was anxious to reach a safe position on shore from which to observe the phenomenon. 'If we should be so fortunate as to Obtain this Observation the Longitude of this place and Country will thereby be very accurately determined.' At 2 p.m. on 3 November 1769, a promising inlet was seen and Cook brought the *Endeavour* to an anchorage near the entrance. Next day the bay was investigated and the ship was worked further in to a more sheltered position about half a mile from the

Plate 38. *"New Zealand War Canoe. The Crew bidding defiance to the Ships Company." Sketch by Herman Spöring on 2 November 1769.*

southern shore. Before long canoes began to collect around the ship. The Maoris seemed friendly and two men were induced to come on board where Cook gave them presents of cloth and spike nails. One of them, an old man named Toiawa, seemed to be a chief.

Cook named this inlet Mercury Bay (plate 39). It proved to be the safest harbour yet discovered and an ideal place to obtain fresh provisions. Birds were plentiful and several black oyster-catchers were shot. The fishing proved disappointing but the Maoris, more expert, provided canoe loads of delicious fish sufficient for the needs of the men and enough when salted to last for more than a month. Wild celery was abundant and boat loads were collected to be 'boild every day for the Ships Compney as usual', while fresh water was readily procured from a small stream which reached the shore about half a mile from the ship (plate 40). The scientists were equally fortunate and Banks wrote in his journal, 'We went ashore and botanizd with our usual good success which could not be doubted in a countrey so totaly new.'

As the visitors moved quietly around the bay the Maoris became bolder and many came aboard the *Endeavour*. Amongst those to visit the ship were several boys one of whom, Te Horeta te Taniwha, was able to recall, many years later, details of Cook's visit to Mercury Bay. The Maoris thought that their visitors were mythical creatures, 'These people are goblins; their eyes are at the back of their heads; they pull on shore with their backs

Plate 39. *Aerial view showing the* Endeavour's *anchorage in Mercury Bay. To the left of the Purangi or Oyster River lies the beach of Cooks Bay from which the transit of Mercury was observed. To the right is the watering place where Cook claimed 'formal possession of the place'. In the background, Wharekaho Beach stretches between the sites of the two Maori pas visited.*

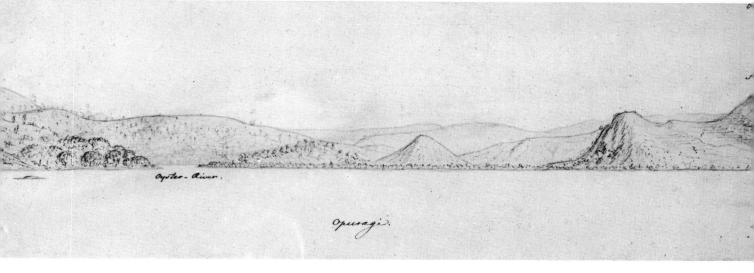

Oyster River.

Opuragi.

Plate 40 (above). *"Opuragi" or Mercury Bay. This sketch by Spöring from the* Endeavour *shows the Oyster River and the beach to the right of it where the observations were made.*

Plate 41 (below). *The observation point on Cooks Beach, Mercury Bay, looking towards the watering place.*

to the land to which they are going'.

Through the eyes of this young Maori lad, who sat with his companions on the deck of the *Endeavour*, we get a vivid impression of James Cook at work. 'There was one supreme man in that ship. We knew that he was the lord of the whole by his perfect gentlemanly and noble demeanour. He seldom spoke, but some of the goblins spoke much. But this man did not utter many words: all that he did was to handle our mats and hold our mere, spears, and waha-ika, and touch the hair of our heads. He was a very good man, and came to us—the children—and patted our cheeks, and gently touched our heads. His language was a hissing sound, and the words he spoke were not understood by us in the least.' Cook then made a speech and asked the chiefs to draw an 'outline of this land'. At last, 'that old man stood up, took the charcoal, and marked the outline of the Ika-a-maui (the North Island of New Zealand). After some time the chief goblin took some white stuff, on which he made a copy of what the old chief had made on the deck, and spoke to the old chief.'

Cook then gave a nail to Te Horeta. 'I took it into my hand and said "Ka pai" (very good), and he repeated my words, and again patted our heads with his hand and went away. My companions said, "This is the leader of the ship, which is proved by his kindness to us; and also he is so very fond of children. A noble man—a rangatira—cannot be lost in the crowd".'

Cook then gave two handfuls of potatoes to the old chief, a gift of profound importance to the

Maoris. By tradition these potatoes were planted at Hunua where, after cultivation for 3 years, a feast was held and a general distribution made.

Fortunately, the sun rose, on 9 November 1769, in a cloudless sky. After an early breakfast Mr Green observed the transit of Mercury from a point on the beach about 300 yards from the mouth of the Oyster or Purangi River (plate 41). Cook seems to have been too busy establishing the exact time to see the early stages of the transit but all observed the egress some 4 hours later. From these observations Mr Green calculated the longitude of the site as being 184° 4′ west of the meridian of Greenwich. The latitude, calculated from the altitude of the sun, was found to be 36° 48′ south of the equator.

Though the method used by the observers to make their estimations is not clear there is no doubt about their accuracy. The position of the observation point at Cooks Bay in Mercury Bay is now computed to be—latitude 36° 50′ 18″ S, and longitude 175° 45′ 23″ E. Measured east of the Greenwich meridian the navigators' longitude was 175° 56′, a difference of about 11 minutes.

While Cook was on shore observing the transit five canoes filled with armed strangers paddled out to the *Endeavour*. Lieutenant Gore, who was in charge of the ship, had traded some cloth for a dogskin cloak, but when this was passed down to the canoe the Maori carefully wrapped the cloth with the cloak and made off shaking his paddle in defiance. Enraged by this insolence Mr Gore shot the offender dead. When Cook returned on board he learned of this encounter, 'but I must own that it did not meet with my approbation because I thought the punishment a little too severe for the Crime, and we had now been long enough acquainted with these People to know how to chastise trifling faults like this without taking away their lives.' Mr Gore's action was, however, in accord with Maori custom and they bore no ill feeling—the man had cheated and with his death had paid the price in blood. They buried him

Plate 42. *Cook's chart of Mercury Bay.*

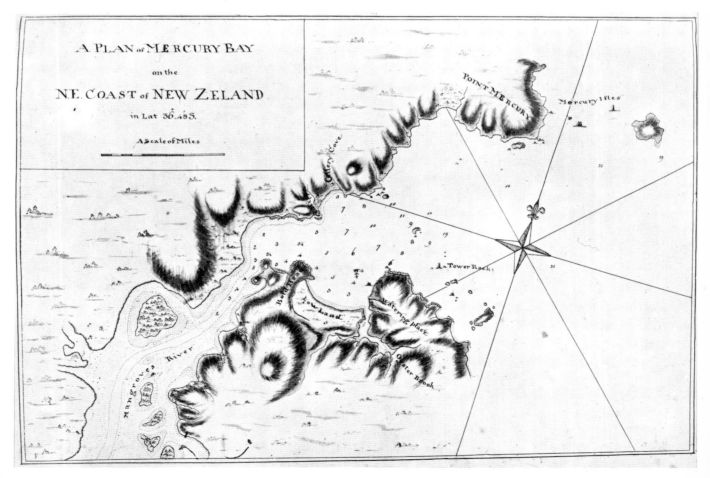

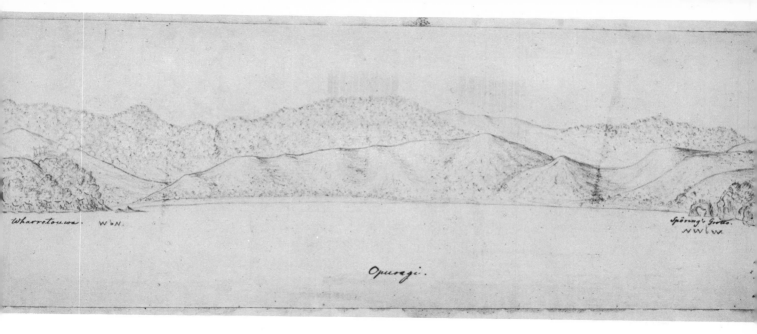

Wharretouwa. W.b.N.   *Spöring's Grotto.*
                                                         N.W.b.W.

Opuragi.

Plate 43.   *This sketch by Spöring looking north from the* Endeavour
*shows the fighting stage of Whare-taewa pa on the left and the
smaller pa, named "Spöring's Grotto", to the right.*

wrapped up in the stolen cloth.

During his stay in Mercury Bay Cook charted the area with his usual accuracy (plate 42). Accompanied by the scientists he ascended the river entering the head of the bay until, about three miles from the mouth, a colony of shags was found nesting in some dead trees. This was the signal for lunch. Banks wrote, 'an attack was consequently made on the Shaggs and about 20 soon killd and as broild and eat, every one declaring that they were excellent food as indeed I think they were. Hunger is certainly most excellent sauce, but since our fowls and ducks have been gone we find ourselves able to eat any kind of Birds (for indeed we throw away none) without even that kind of seasoning.' The river near the watering place was also explored and found to contain extensive beds of oysters. In no time the long boat was loaded down to the gunwale with 'as good oysters as ever came from Colchester'.

But before leaving the bay Cook was anxious to inspect more closely a palisaded village, or 'hippa' about which structures there had been so much speculation during the voyage along the coast. Accordingly, on Monday, 3 November 1769, accompanied by the scientists he took the pinnace and the yawl across the bay to the northern shore (plate 43), being rather uncertain of the reception

he was likely to receive. Going first to the smaller of the two pas which was situated on a rock at the eastern end of 'Cellery Cove', the visitors were relieved to be welcomed by friendly natives who invited them to come ashore. Banks was delighted at the little pa which he described as 'the most beautifuly romantick thing I ever saw'. It was built on a small but high rock detached from the mainland, 'but what made it most truly romantick was that much the largest part of it was hollowd out into an arch which penetrated quite through it and was in hight not less than 20 yards perpendicular above the water which ran through it'. The Maori name for this unusual fortification was Te Puta o Paretauhinau—The Hole of Paretauhinau, and the sailors called it Spöring's Grotto. The artists were quick to sketch it (plate 44).

It is sad to report that this rock has been gradually eroded by time and tide. A sketch made in 1870 shows the arch still complete, although its flat top had been reduced to a narrow spine. Today only the pillars remain as, at some time, the rest has crashed into the seabed below. However, the little beach to the right, on which the artists showed two canoes, still marks the site of this picturesque pa (plate 45).

The party, now wishing to inspect the larger pa at the western end of 'Cellery Cove', rowed over

Plate 44. *"View of an Indian Fortification built upon an Arched Rock in Mercury Bay." By J. Cook.*

Plate 45. *The remains of the "Arched Rock" in 1969. The centre has collapsed.*

to the beach and landed about a mile from the village. They walked along the shore escorted by about 100 men, women and children who took them to their stronghold called Whare-taewa (plate 46). Banks described it thus—'It was calld Wharretoowa and was situate on the end of a hill where it Jutted out into the sea which washd two sides of it, these were sufficiently steep but not absolutely inaccessible; up one of the land sides which was also steep went the road, the other was flat and open to the side of the hill. The whole was inclosd by a pallisade about 10 feet high made of strong pales bound together with withs; the weak side next the hill had also a ditch the face of which next the pallisade we measurd to be 20½ feet in depth. Besides this over the pallisade was built a fighting stage which they call Porava, which is a flat stage coverd with boughs of trees upon which they stand to throw darts or stones at their assailants out of danger of their weapons. The dimensions of it were thus: the hight from the ground 20½ feet, breadth 6 ft 6, the lengh 43 feet. Upon it were laid bundles of darts and heaps of stones ready in case of an attack.'

To demonstrate their method of fighting two of the young men gladly agreed to take part in a mock battle, singing their war songs and threatening each other with their frightful gesticulations and menacing use of their weapons. Banks also noted the 'vast heaps of Dryd fish and fern roots' which were stored in the pa in case of emergency.

Cook was also impressed by the strength of the fortification. 'Upon the whole I looked up [on] it to be a very strong and well choose post and where a small number of resolute men might defend them selves a long time against a vast superior force, Arm'd in the manner as these people are.' But he shrewdly detected a weakness in the defences,

Plate 46. *Aerial view looking over the site of Whare-taewa pa, and along Wharekaho Beach past the Ake Ake River to "Spöring's Grotto".*

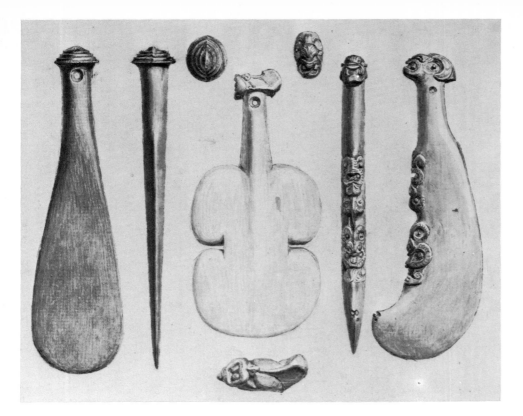

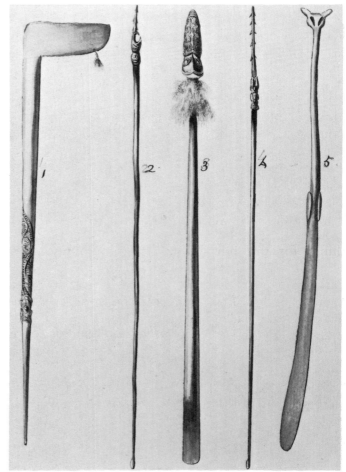

'but we did not see that they had any fresh water nearer then a brook which runs close under the foot of the hill, from which I suppose they can at times get Water, tho beseiged and keep it in Gourds untill they use it.'

It was, in fact, the shortage of water which led to the reduction of the pa some 30 years later by Ngatihei warriors under Te Rangi-anini, who cut the water supply and, after a siege of several weeks, took the stronghold with great slaughter. Some, however, escaped to two rocky islets off the point mentioned by Cook, 'they are both very small and more fit for birds to inhabit than men yet there are houses and places of defence on each of them.' (plate 49).

There could now be no doubt concerning the warlike character of the Maoris whose very existence depended on the strength of their defensive strongholds and their skill in hand to hand fighting. Though he was surprised at the absence of bows and arrows, and slings, Cook was greatly impressed by the skilful use of the weapons they had evolved. He described them thus. 'The Arms they use are Long spears or lances [huata], a Staff about 5 feet long, some of these are pointed at one end like a Serjeants Halbard [taiaha] others round and sharp [pouwhenua], the other ends are broad something

like the blade of an oar; they have another sort about 4½ feet long, these are shaped at one end like an Axe and the other is made with a sharp point [tewhatewha]; they have short Truncheons about a foot long, which they call Patto Pattoos [patu], some made of wood some of bone and others of stone, those made of wood are variously shaped, but those made of bone and stone are of one shape, which is with a round handle a broadish blade which is thickest in the middle and tapers to an edge all round, the use of these are to knock mens brains out and to kill them outright after they are wounded: and they are certainly well contrived things for this purpose (plate 47). Besides these weapons they throw stones and darts [pere], the darts are 10 or 12 feet long, are made of hard wood and are barb'd at one end. They handle all their arms with great Agility particularly their long Pikes or Lances (plate 48), against which we have no weapon that is an equal match except a loaded Musquet.'

The position of these two pas may be seen by studying Pickersgill's chart and Spöring's sketch. They lie at each end of Wharekaho, or Simpson's, Beach on the northern shore of Mercury Bay. Near the seaward end of this beach the 'Cellery', or Ake Ake River enters the bay. The site of

Whare-taewa pa may still be recognised at the southern extremity of Wharekaho Beach. The position of the earthworks which once defended the landward approaches may just be discerned and the Tohetea Stream still meanders down the valley at the foot of the hill. The countryside is now well-grassed except for a coastal fringe of bush which survives where the cliffs rise steeply from the sea. A few pohutukawa trees, dotted through the fields, provide shelter for the sheep and cattle too lazy, in the heat of summer, to venture far from their shade. These few trees are all that remain of the forests which provided Cook's naturalists with 'an enormous number' of plants new to science.

One more duty remained for the men of the *Endeavour*. 'Before we left this Bay,' wrote Cook, 'we cut out upon one of the trees near the watering place, the Ships Name, date &ca and after displaying the English Colours I took formal possession of the place in the name of His Majesty.' Cook had then been on the New Zealand coast for 6 weeks and it has surprised many that he did not make any territorial claims at an earlier date. The Admiralty's instructions, however, stated—'You are also with the Consent of the Natives to take possession of Convenient Situations in the Country in the Name of the King of Great Britain', and it

Plate 50 (left). *The stream where Cook filled his water casks in Mercury Bay.*

Plate 51 (below). *Looking out across Mercury Bay towards Shakespeare Cliff. Cook raised the Union flag at the watering place, probably where the figures are standing on the little hill surrounded by pohutukawa trees.*

may well be that Cook felt he could not claim 'the Consent of the Natives' until he had been able to establish reasonably amicable relations with them and that Mercury Bay afforded the first 'Convenient Situation'.

The little stream which provided the *Endeavour* with fresh water tumbles down a secluded valley into the bay about 200 yards east of the mouth of the Purangi River. There is an air of anonymity about this important place and even the stream remains nameless. It rises in the highlands behind Cook Bluff—the headland which guards the southern entrance to Mercury Bay—and descends, in the latter part of its journey, by steps and stairs providing clear pools which must have made the filling of water casks an easy matter (plate 50). Just south of the place where the stream enters the sea there is a flat area about 20 feet above high-water mark. It is a pleasant knoll surrounded by pohutukawa trees and looking out on Cook's

Plate 52. Podocarpus spicatus *or Matai. This specimen was collected near the Thames River in November 1769 when Sydney Parkinson sketched it. F. P. Nodder made this painting in 1780 from the sketch.*

anchorage. Though it might not be easy of access, this plot, where Cook first raised the British flag, seems worthy of greater attention (plate 51).

At 7 a.m. on 15 November 1769, the anchor was weighed and the *Endeavour* sailed out of the harbour, past Tower Rock, before a light westerly breeze. Soon, however, squally gales lashed the ship and Cook prudently worked to the north, outside the Mercury Islands. It was 4 days later before he was able to round a bold rocky promontory, which he named after his old friend and commander Lord Colville, to enter the quiet waters of a bay which seemed to penetrate deeply into the land to the southward. As the ship coasted along the eastern shore of this bay several canoes paddled out to the *Endeavour*, for news of her had already reached the Maoris. Cook wrote in his journal, 'several of the People came on board upon the very first invitation; this was owing to their having heard of our being upon the Coast and the manner we had treated the Natives. I made each of those that came on board a small present. . . .' The Maoris, not to be outdone, gave the visitors a large parcel of smoked eels which, according to Parkinson, tasted 'very sweet' and luscious'.

Cook sailed the ship as far as he dared towards the head of the bay and anchored in 6 fathoms about 9 miles from what appeared to be a large river. This seemed to offer a good opportunity to see 'a little of the Interior parts of the Country and its produce'. Accordingly, at daybreak next morning, 20 November 1769, accompanied by Banks, Solander and Tupaia, Cook set off with the pinnace and the long boat and reached the river mouth at the beginning of the flood tide. This river was 'as wide as the River Thames at Greenwich', though shallower, and the strength of the tides reminded him of the lower reaches of that river in England from which he had sailed 16 months before.

As they ascended rapidly with the tide, mangrove swamps soon gave way to stately stands of kauri and kahikatea or white pine. Joseph Banks noted that 'the banks of the river were compleatly cloathd with the finest timber my Eyes ever beheld', and Cook recognised immediately its value to the ship building trade. They landed on the west bank some 12 miles from the sea to measure one of these trees. Cook wrote, 'we had not gone a hundred yards into the Woods before we found a tree that girted 19 feet 8 Inches 6 feet above the Ground, and having a quadrant with me I found its length from the root to the first branch to be 89 feet, it was as streight as an arrow and taper'd but very little in proportion to its length, so that I judged that there was 356 solid feet of timber in this tree clear of the branches. We saw many others of the same sort several of which were taller than the one we measured and all of them very stout; there were likewise many other sorts of very stout timber-trees all of them wholy unknown to any of us.' Maori tradition identifies the tree which Cook had measured as a kahikatea which grew on the west bank of the river near Hikutaia. It was felled for milling just before 1900, and its measurements tallied exactly with those given by Cook.

Impossible to climb and with their branches high above the ground, the identification of these huge trees presented a difficult problem which Banks attempted to solve by cutting down a young specimen growing beneath them. In the event, he seems to have selected a different, though similar species from that measured by Cook. It was a black pine or matai from a branch of which Parkinson probably made a drawing (plate 52). Its wood was judged to be too heavy and solid for masts or spars but ideal for planking. Time had passed quickly in the forest. 'We brought away a few specimens', wrote Cook, 'and at 3 oClock we embarqued in order to return on board with the very first of the Ebb, but not before we had named this the Thames on account of its bearing some resemblence to that river in england.'

On the way down river the natives met the party again in the 'most friendly manner immagineable' and the sea was reached without incident. Here, however, the turn of the tide and a strong head wind made it impossible to reach the ship and the night was spent in some discomfort riding at anchor in showers of rain.

The enthusiastic description of these timber trees brought Captain Dell, in the Fancy, to the Thames River from Port Jackson 25 years later, in 1794–95, seeking spars for the East India Company's naval vessels. He landed sawyers and an Indian guard near the mouth of the river thus initiating one of the first commercial ventures in New Zealand which, in little more than 100 years, destroyed the magnificent forest which had made such an impression on the explorers. Ordered farmlands now extend out from the banks of the River Thames as it snakes its way to the sea. The swamps have been drained but a few patches of mangroves still grow along the shore and on the low islands in the river. Of the great forest nothing now remains (plate 53).

Next day the anchor was weighed with the ebb tide but, without a breeze, progress was slow. While Cook and Solander took the opportunity to explore the western shore in the pinnace, several of the natives came aboard and were trading fairly when one of them stole the half-minute glass★ from the binnacle, and was caught in the act. Mr Hicks punished the offender with 'a Dozn lashes with a Catt of nine tails' with the approval of the other Maoris, once Tupaia had explained what the whipping was for—in fact, a second beating was administered soon after by an old man, possibly his father, before they all returned to the

★This measured half-minute intervals and, used in conjunction with the log-line enabled the speed of the ship to be determined. It was therefore an important aid to navigation.

Plate 53. *Aerial view of the Thames River. Maori tradition identifies the position of the tree which Cook measured as growing within the nearest loop of the river. This lies to the west of the township of Hikutaia.*

shore. Relations with the Maori people had certainly changed since the first landing 6 weeks before.

Without wind, progress to the north was limited to what could be made on the outgoing tide but, by 9 p.m. on the evening of 23 November 1769, a position near the north-east point of Waiheke Island was reached and the anchor dropped. While drifting along the Firth of Thames which he had included in his 'River Thames', Cook noticed some good harbours on the eastern shore. He also mapped portions of the coastline of Ponui, Waiheke, and Rangitoto Islands to the west and noted that

'it appear'd very probable that these form'd some good harbours likewise'. Weighing anchor at 3 a.m. next morning his chance of discovering the sheltered waters of the Waitemata Harbour on the shores of which the city of Auckland now stands gradually vanished in the grey light of dawn.

A strong gale from the south-west carried the *Endeavour* northward in the shelter of the Barrier Isles until 7.30 p.m. on Saturday, 24 November 1769, when the anchor was dropped in a wide bay. Here nearly 100 bream or tarakihi were soon hauled on board, an event perpetuated by

Plate 54 (at top). *"Cape Brett & Piercy Island." Sketched from the* Endeavour *by Herman Spöring.*

Plate 55 (above). *Cape Brett and Piercy Island, 1969.*

Cook in the name of the bay and the headlands to the north and south of it—Bream Head and Bream Tail. Setting sail again at daybreak Cook noted the remarkable 'peeked rocks' rainged in order' on the top of Bream Head, but failed to discern in the early light the entrance to Whangarei Harbour to the westward of it.

Several groups of natives visited the *Endeavour* as she sailed along the coast. Most of them were heavily tattooed on the buttocks and thighs as well as on the body and face. Nothing would induce them to sell their valued greenstone or whalebone patu, but otherwise trading was brisk. Not all

the negotiations ended smoothly, however, as Banks has recorded, 'In the afternoon other Canoes came off and from some inattention of the officers were sufferd to cheat unpunishd and unfrightned. This put one of the Midshipmen who had sufferd upon a droll tho rather mischeivous revenge. He got a fishing line and when the Canoe was close to the ship hove the lead at the man who had cheated, with so good success that he fastned the hook into his backside, on which he pulld with all his might and the Indian kept back, so the hook soon broke in the shank leaving its beard in his backside, no very agreable legacy.'

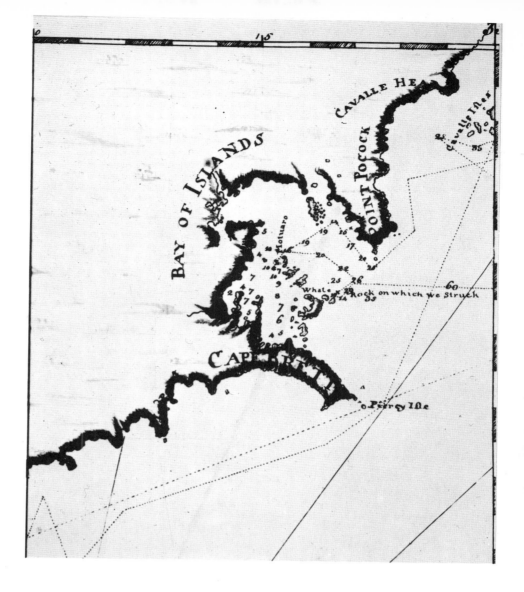

Plate 56. *Map of the Bay of Islands by J. Cook shows the track of the* Endeavour.

At this time the *Endeavour* was approaching a bold headland which Cook, in whimsical mood, named Cape Brett (plates 54 and 55) in honour of Rear-Admiral Sir Piercy Brett, one of the three Lords of the Admiralty who had signed his secret instructions. For, lying off the point, was a rocky island 'with a hole perced quite thro' it like the Arch of a Bridge and this was one reason why I gave the Cape the above name because *Piercy* seem'd very proper for that of the Island'.

On rounding Cape Brett the *Endeavour* sailed across the entrance of a large, deep bay where there were many islands. Several villages were seen and

a great number of canoes put out from the shore. It was estimated that during the day no less than 400 or 500 natives came alongside or boarded the ship. Cook was struck with their appearance, 'all stout well made men, having all of them their hair which was black Comb'd up and tied upon the Crown of their heads and there stuck with white feathers.' In each of the canoes were several chiefs dressed in cloaks 'of the best sort and cover'd on the outside with Dog skins put on in such a manner as to look agreeable enough to the Eye'. But Parkinson was less favourably impressed with their behaviour, 'while I saluted one of them, in

Plate 57. *From the* Endeavour's *anchorage Spöring drew three pictures of Motu Arohia in panoramic form. The left-hand sketch shown here identifies the beach where the first landing was made.*

Plate 58. *Aerial view of the Bay of Islands. Motu Arohia lies across the foreground with Moturua behind it and Cape Brett in the distance.*

Motuaro.   The Heppa.   NE.

Plate 59. *The right-hand sketch of Motu Arohia by Herman Spöring shows the hill climbed by Banks and the Maori pa on its eastern point.*

their manner, he picked my pocket'. Indeed, after continual threatening they began an attack with stones to such effect that it was necessary to open fire with small shot to discourage them.

Bad weather forced the *Endeavour* off shore and, after several days of fruitless tacking into the teeth of a north-westerly gale off the Cavalli Islands, Cook decided to seek shelter and gain some further knowledge of the country. And so, on 29 November 1769, the ship entered the Bay of Islands (plate 56) and anchored 'under the SW side of one of the many Islands' at 11 o'clock in the morning. It was decided to land on this island, called Motu Arohia and, as the natives seemed hostile, Cook took precautions. With an armed guard and in company with the scientists he took the pinnace and the yawl about ¾ mile to a sandy beach, clearly identified by Spöring in his sketch (plate 57).

No sooner had the party landed than it was surrounded by several hundred armed Maoris who advanced in a menacing fashion. An ugly situation was relieved only by the resolution of Cook and the scientists who stood firm and fired small shot at the leaders, the discipline of the guard who withheld their musket fire, and the quick thinking of Mr Hicks who, sensing an attack, quickly brought the *Endeavour's* guns to bear and fired a broadside of 4-pound cannonballs over the heads of the attacking warriors. The balance between

success and disaster in such an encounter is fine indeed and it must have been with relief that they all laid down their muskets and gathered 'celery' for next morning's breakfast.

Later the boats were rowed to another beach on the same island where Cook and the scientists climbed a hill to get a good view of the bay (plate 58). The scene which unfolded was thus described by Banks—'the bay we were in was indeed a most surprizing place: it was full of an innumerable quantity of Islands forming as many harbours, which must be as smooth as mill pools as they Landlock one another numberless times.' The intricate pattern of these islands discouraged Cook from making a detailed survey of this extensive harbour and, as time was precious, he contented himself by observing, 'I thought it quite sufficient to be able to affirm with certainty that it affords good anchorage and every kind of refreshments for Shipping.'

The area of the Bay of Islands which Cook visited is that part cradled between the peninsula which points like a finger north and east into the Pacific, and which is tipped by Cape Brett, and Tapeka Point which protects the head of the bay, behind which nestles the little town of Russell and, across the water, Paihia. It was the seaward aspect of Tapeka Point and the islands lying between it and Cape Brett, which were best

Plate 60. *Drawing of the Maori pa built on the eastern tip of Motu Arohia, probably by Sydney Parkinson.*

Plate 61. *Pine trees are now growing on the site of this pa.*

Plate 62.　*Waipao Bay on Moturua. The stream from which Cook obtained water may be seen at the edge of the sandy beach in the right lower foreground.*

known to the men of the *Endeavour*. The outermost islands, Okahu, Waewaetorea and Urapuka-puka, form a bulwark which protects those within from the easterly winds and waves. Inside the bulwark lies Motukiekie and then the larger island of Moturua, on which is the sandy bay where both Cook, and Marion du Fresne 3 years later, found fresh water. Still further in lies the island called Motu Arohia* which was the scene of Cook's first landing.

The name of this island has always been troublesome. Some of the *Endeavour's* men in an attempt to provide a phonetic spelling wrote 'Cumatti-warroweia'—which Banks analysed as—'Ko Motu-aro aheiha, it is Motu-aro, truly'. It was labelled thus on the sketch Spöring made from the deck of the *Endeavour* as she lay at anchor.

He was confined to the ship while Cook and his party were testing the temper of the Maori

inhabitants of the bay, but he did not waste his time. He completed a panorama, which consisted of three separate drawings of Motu Arohia. The accuracy of his draughtsmanship allows us to pinpoint the position of the *Endeavour* and identifies, with certainty, the places of historical interest. When the three sketches are aligned, that on the left depicts the western bay, under which is written—'Here we landed'. The middle sketch illustrates the second landing place on a curved sandy beach backed by rocky pinnacles; while the right hand, or third section of the panorama shows the rounded hill climbed by Banks, in order to see the bay beyond, and includes the island's easterly point on which stood a Maori pa (plate 59). This sketch identifies the fortification which was the subject of Parkinson's well-known drawing (plate 60). Today there are windswept pine trees where once the palisades held off the attacks of hostile warriors. (plate 61).

Cook made an attempt to leave this quiet anchorage on the next morning, 30 November

*Today it is variously referred to as Brown's, Robinson's or Roberton's Island as well as by its official name.

Plate 63. *Aerial view of the Orokawa Peninsula. The Maori gardens were situated on the flat area and the pas on the wooded headlands. Several houses at the base of the peninsula mark Assassination Cove in Te Hue Bay where Marion du Fresne and his party were killed.*

1769, but the wind soon died and he was forced to anchor again. As there was little fresh water on Motu Arohia he took a boat over to the island of Moturua and landed on a sandy beach, known as Waipao Bay, where there were two small streams (plate 62). Later this beach was to be the site of the hospital and forge erected by Marion du Fresne during his ill-fated visit in 1772.

On Monday, 4 December 1769, Cook and his scientists rowed over to the 'Main' (plate 63). On their way they passed a point of land on which stood a pa and they were invited ashore by the Maoris. Banks and Solander were very interested to see the extensive gardens of sweet potato and yam and, for the first time in New Zealand, half a dozen aute, or paper mulberry trees from which the Maoris made cloth in exactly the same way as it was made in Tahiti. The village was a little way from the pa and the countryside was 'full of small hills and Vallies' which were 'not very much incumber'd with wood'. This description seems to

refer to the Orokawa Peninsula and the village was probably that mentioned later by Marion du Fresne as 'Tacoury's village'.

But what impressed them most was the skill of the Maoris in catching fish and the equipment they used for this purpose. Cook's men could catch only a few fish but fortunately they were able to purchase great quantities from the natives, which were caught in 'prodigious large' nets. Banks wrote—'after having a little laugh at our seine, which was a common kings seine, shewd us one of theirs which was 5 fathom [30 feet] deep and its length we could only guess, as it was not stretchd out, but it could not from its bulk be less than 4 or 500 fathom [$\frac{1}{2}$ mile]. Fishing seems to be the cheif business of this part of the countrey; about all their towns are abundance of netts laid upon small heaps like hay cocks and thatchd over and almost every house you go into has netts in it making.' Such a net or kaharoa was the joint work and property of the whole village.

It was made of strips of green flax joined together by a weaver's knot. Usually a finger was used to gauge the size of the mesh but sometimes mesh gauges made of wood or whalebone were employed. In seine nets the mesh at the ends was made larger than that in the middle of the net.

Next morning, on 5 December 1769, another attempt was made to get under way but the wind soon dropped and the ship was left drifting helplessly with the current near the islands of the bay. At 10 p.m. the waves were breaking on the lee shore less than a cable's length from the ship while Tupaia, not realising the danger of the situation, was conversing with the Maoris on the beach. Shipwreck was averted at the last moment 'by the help of our boat and a light air from the southward' to the great relief of the ship's company. But the danger was not yet over. Banks wrote in his journal, 'We were all happy in our breeze and fine clear moonlight; myself went down to bed and sat upon my cott undressing myself when I felt the ship strike upon a rock, before I could get upon my leggs she struck again. I ran upon deck but before I could get there the danger was over; fortunately the rock was to wind ward of us so she went off without the least damage and we got into the proper channel, where the officers who had examind the bay declard there to be no hidden dangers—much to our satisfaction as the almost certainty of being eat as soon as you come ashore adds not a little to the terrors of shipwreck.' This rock which Cook called Whale Rock is sometimes known as Te Nunuhe Rock (plate 56). It lies about $\frac{1}{2}$ mile north-west of Okahu Island and in calm weather its position is disclosed only by a lumpiness in the water, though the rock breaks white in a running sea.

Once again the Endeavour had reached the open sea and, moving slowly north, Cook reached Doubtless Bay on 9 December 1769. A series of vicious westerly gales now began to batter the ship and all aboard were grateful to the faithful ship-builders of Whitby. Banks wrote, 'we turned all day without loosing any thing, much to the credit of our old Collier, who we never fail to praise if she turns as well as this.'

By a strange coincidence Cook sailed close to the Saint Jean Baptiste under Jean de Surville, about midday on 15 December 1769, without sighting her. On a voyage destined to end in Peru, Surville was driving in front of a westerly storm 20 or 30 miles off North Cape while Cook was beating against the wind 30 miles still further north. Sailing south, the Frenchman sheltered in Doubtless Bay just one week after Cook had passed its entrance.

By 24 December 1769, Cook had reached and recognised the Three Kings Islands charted by Tasman on 6 January 1643, and a special celebration seemed to be indicated. In a lull in the storm Banks managed to shoot several gannets—'as it was the humour of the ship to keep Christmas in the old fashion way.' The party was a success as his entry next day recorded. 'Christmas day: Our Goose pye was eat with great approbation and in the Evening all hands were as Drunk as our fore-fathers usd to be upon the like occasion.'

It was now Cook's plan to follow Tasman's track along the coast in the reverse direction to determine if possible whether or not Cape Maria van Diemen marked a northern extension of the Southern Continent. But this was not to be easy sailing. For many days the Endeavour was blasted by winds of exceptional violence. Even the laconic Cook wrote—'it was a meer hurricane attended with rain and the Sea run prodigious high.' Although hove to under close-reefed topsails, 'the SW Sea runs so high that the Ship goes boddily to leeward', and, after struggling for a week the sailors had the mortification of seeing once again the outline of Cape Maria van Diemen.

The new year began with more promise but Cook dared not take his ship too close to that forbidding shore. He wrote 'the great sea which the prevailing westerly winds impell upon the Shore must render this a very dangerous Coast, this I am so fully sencible of that was we once clear of it I am determind not to come so near again if I can possible avoide it unless we have a very favourable wind indeed.'

By Sunday, 7 January 1770, the wind had dropped and a course was set for the south once more in calm pleasant weather. A turtle dived and swam to safety as the Endeavour glided past and Banks was able to shoot several different species of sea bird to add to his collection. Off Hokianga Harbour a large sun fish was seen, described by Sydney Parkinson as 'very short and thick, having scarce any tail, but two large fins; it was as big as a shark, and of the same colour'.

Sailing parallel with the coast Cook passed the entrance to Raglan Harbour on 10 January 1770, with the depth of water between 34 and 48 fathoms and a black sandy bottom. The Endeavour sailed just inside an island, that according to Banks

Plate 64. *Mount Egmont from the sea.*

'seemd almost totaly coverd with birds probably Gannets', which would have been nesting at that time. On that account it was named Gannet Island. Banks was much impressed by the appearance of the coast. 'The countrey we passd by appeard fertile, more so I think than any part of this countrey I have seen, rising in gentle slopes not over wooded but what trees there were well grown. Few signs of inhabitants were seen, a fire and a very few houses'.

In the evening light a very high peaked mountain could be faintly seen on the southern horizon. This proved to be the centre of interest for the next 3 days while the *Endeavour* sailed slowly around its western side. For the most part concealed by cloud its head appeared for tantalisingly brief intervals. On Saturday, 13 January 1770 Cook wrote, 'At 5 AM saw for a few Minutes the Top of the peaked Mountain above the Clowds, bearing NE; it is of a prodigious height and its top is cover'd with everlasting snow'. It was likened by the sailors to the well known volcanic cone of Tenerife and its height was a matter for much speculation. Banks did not hazard a guess but remarked, 'it is certainly the noblest hill I have ever seen and it appears to the utmost advantage rising from the sea without another hill in its neighbourhood one 4th part of its hight'. Before the peak was enveloped by a heavy thunderstorm Parkinson noted that its sides were covered with trees, and Banks, through his glasses, was able to distinguish 'many white lumps in companies of 50 or 60 together which probably were either stones or tufts of grass but bore much the resemblance of flocks of sheep'.

Cook named this striking peak Mount Egmont in honour of John Perceval, second Earl of Egmont, who was First Lord of the Admiralty from 1763 to 1766. It rises in isolation to 8,260 feet, is an extinct volcano, and even in mid-summer carries a little snow on its top (plate 64).

The *Endeavour* was now running into a large bay clearly marked on Tasman's map (plate 66). Cook was anxious to find a harbour suitable for careening the ship, where repairs could be carried out and where wood and fresh provisions could be procured. Keeping a sharp lookout he noticed Kapiti Island (which he later named Entry Island) about 5 leagues distant against the eastern shore, but, directly to the south, he saw no land. 'The bottom of the Bay we are now in, and which bears from us south, we cannot see, altho it is very clear in that quarter.'

In the evening a possible harbour was seen to the south-west and Cook tacked back and forth outside it all night. At daylight however, according to Banks, 'we were drove to the Eastward more than we had any reason to expect, so much that we found ourselves in the morn past the harbour we intended to go into. Another however was in sight into which we went: the land on both sides appeard most miserably barren till we got pretty deep in when it began to mend by gradual degrees'. Soon after entering this bay (plate 65) the *Endeavour* was again caught in a strong current setting to the north-west and was only kept off a ledge of rocks by the efforts of the towing boats.

By noon the ship had reached an island called Motuara, near the centre of the channel and about 7 miles from the entrance. Many armed natives shouted defiance and brandished their weapons as the *Endeavour* was towed round the south-western point on which stood a village or 'hippa'.★ By 2 p.m. on Tuesday, 15 January 1770, the ship had reached a 'very snug Cove' on the north-west side of the bay and Cook dropped the stream anchor in 11 fathoms of water.

This was Ship Cove. From the deck of the *Endeavour* Cook could see past Motuara to the entrance of the bay. Remembering the gap in the coastline and the treacherous currents there, he suspected a passage to the 'Eastern Sea'. He was determined to find it.

★The European version of 'he pa'—the pa.

Plate 65. *Aerial view of Queen Charlotte Sound looking over East Bay and Long Point towards the entrance. The* Endeavour *sailed past Cape Jackson (top right) and between Long Island and Motuara before anchoring in Ship Cove, in the upper left background.*

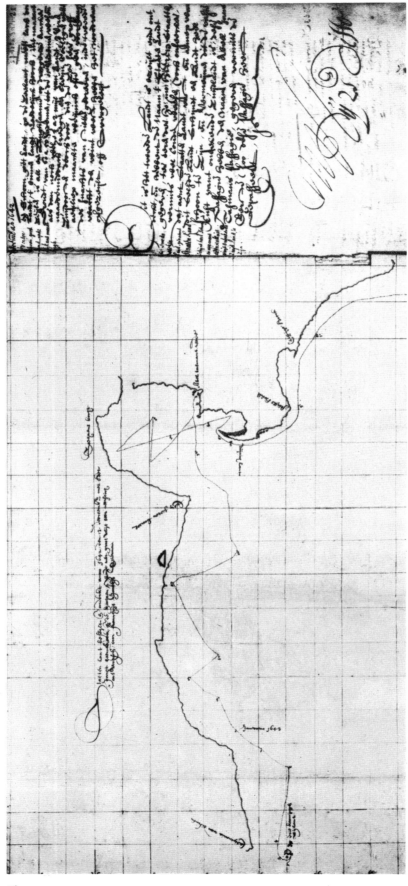

Plate 66. *This map was drawn by Franchoys Jacobszoon Visscher during Tasman's voyage to New Zealand in 1642–43. A gap in the coastline marks the northern entry into Cook Strait. The notes beside the map, written in 17th century Dutch, describe the country which was named Staten Land. Translated, a section of the second paragraph reads, "This land seems to be very beautiful and we trust that it is the main coastline of the unknown South Land".*

4 Cook Strait

*The captn went to the top of a hill and in about an
hour returnd in high spirits, having seen the Eastern sea
and satisfied himself of the existence of a streight com-
municating with it*

Joseph Banks

Abel Tasman, in 1642, made his landfall off the rugged west coast of the South Island and sailed north wondering if this high land was an extension of the southern continent. His ships soon entered what appeared to be a huge bay bounded on the south by Cape Farewell and the crenellated coast of the South Island, and to the north by Cape Egmont and the curving shores of the North Island. He had established that there was a break in the western coastline of New Zealand but had not determined whether it was merely a deep indentation or a seaway which led to the Pacific Ocean.

James Cook, approaching from the north, was confronted with the same situation. If it was a bay the continental theory could still be maintained and it would be necessary to examine the position further by beating down the west coast against the prevailing winds along a dangerous lee shore. If there was a strait, however, the land he had just explored was not continuous with the southern continent, and he could proceed to the south along a coast protected from the fierce westerly winds. It was a problem of considerable importance and its solution would either greatly strengthen or severely damage the arguments of the 'Continentalists'.

Tasman, commanding the *Heemskerck* and accompanied by the *Zeehaen* had been rebuffed, after he had entered the bay, in a surprise attack by its warlike inhabitants. As four men had been killed he decided to sail east in search of water and refreshments. On 20 December 1642, Tasman found himself surrounded by a very beautiful land which he thought might be the mainland coast of the unknown South Land. He noted in his journal, 'The sea ran very strongly into this bay, so that we could make no headway. Drifted back into the bay with the current.' In addition, he seems to have seen what might have been an opening to the south. Franchoys Jacobszoon Visscher, his chief pilot who was noted for his careful charting, shows this on his map (plate 66). However, a series of vicious gales forced the ships to shelter in Abel Tasman's Reede (now Admiralty Bay) until 24 December 1642 when the wind dropped (plate 67). A conference was held on the *Heemskerck* and Tasman suggested that 'since the tide was running from the south-east, there might be a through passage' which could be investigated as soon as the wind and weather allowed. But on Christmas Day the weather 'still looked dark' and next morning it was decided to sail to the north leaving the issue in doubt.

The problem still remained unsolved when, 127 years later, Cook anchored the *Endeavour* in Ship Cove. It must have been tantalizing for him to see the high hills to the east which effectively blocked his view of the seaway which lay beyond.

Before Cook could investigate this geographical problem he had more urgent matters requiring attention. Ship Cove seemed to offer all that he needed (plate 68). As soon as the *Endeavour* was anchored he and the scientists rowed to the bottom of the cove and found a fine stream of excellent water, the hills were covered with timber suitable for repairing the ship, a few hauls of the seine produced 300 pounds of fish, many shags were shot for food and 'scurvy grass' was plentiful along the shore. Though Cook was delighted, the scientists were disappointed at finding only two new plants during the whole evening.

Plate 67 (above). *Abel Tasman's Reede.* Tasman anchored his ships in this roadstead in December 1642 between the Rangitoto Islands in the foreground and D'Urville Island beyond.

Plate 68 (left). *Ship Cove in Queen Charlotte Sound.*

Next morning, 16 January 1770, work on the ship began. She was careened, scrubbed and caulked. The carpenters set about making good the storm damage, the coopers began to mend the empty casks and a forge was set up on shore to repair, once more, the tiller braces.

This busy scene was watched by about a hundred natives who had paddled into the cove in three canoes. They seemed quite friendly and were willing to trade their fish and discuss with Tupaia the legends of their ancestors. The women and some of the men wore a novel head-dress of black feathers which Banks thought rather attractive (plate 69). 'On seeing this my Judgement paid an involuntary compliment to my fair English countrey women; for led astray by this head dress which in some measure resembles their high foretops I was forward to declare it as my opinion that these were much the hansomest women we had seen upon the coast, but upon their nearer approach I was convinced that nothing but the head dress had misled me as I saw not one who was even tolerably hansome.' Parkinson made some delightful sketches of the Maoris wearing these unusual feather hats.

Plate 69. *Two Maori men and two women sketched by Parkinson when their canoes visited the* Endeavour *in Ship Cove. Some wore unusual hats made of black feathers*.

That it must have been a sign of mourning was soon to become clear for, while Cook, Banks and Tupaia were exploring the shore about a mile nearer the entrance of the bay, they came across a family of Maoris cooking their evening meal. A dog was being baked in their oven but many of the provision baskets nearby contained human bones from which the flesh had been partly eaten. Although the Maoris had made no secret of the fact that they were in the habit of eating their enemies slain in combat, this was the first occasion when real evidence of cannibalism had been seen. As the details of the feast were related to Tupaia a translation was made. Banks wrote, 'The horrour that apeard in the countenances of the seamen on hearing this discourse which was immediately translated for the good of the company is better conceivd than describd.' But the Maoris saw nothing wrong with the practice and readily took a forearm, as described by Cook, 'and to shew us that they had eat the flesh they bit a[nd] naw'd the bone and draw'd it thro their mouth and this in such a manner as plainly shew'd that the flesh to them was a dainty bit'. Not surprisingly this place was named Cannibal Bay.

Next morning, however, the horror of the previous night was forgotten and Banks wrote in his journal on 17 January 1770, 'This morn I was awakd by the singing of the birds ashore from whence we are distant not a quarter of a mile, the numbers of them were certainly very great who seemd to strain their throats with emulation perhaps; their voices were certainly the most melodious wild musick I have ever heard, almost imitating small bells but with the most tuneable silver sound imaginable to which may be the distance was no small addition.' Fortunately the dawn chorus may still be enjoyed in this area though the number of bellbirds has been sadly reduced by the wholesale destruction of the bush.

During the next few days Cook and the scientists made several expeditions in the pinnace to survey

Plate 70. *"New Zealanders Fishing." A pen and wash drawing by Sydney Parkinson. These Maori fishermen at Queen Charlotte Sound, in their feather hats, were much more successful than the Europeans.*

the shores of this extensive inlet. They found the western shore well wooded but the eastern very bare. On rounding a point one day, they came upon a Maori fishing from a small canoe. A true fisherman, he continued unconcernedly with his task and was only too pleased to demonstrate his method. 'On our desiring him he took up his netts and shewd us his machine,' wrote Banks, 'which was a circular net about 7 or 8 feet in diameter extended by 2 hoops; the top of this was open and to the bottom was tied sea Ears &c. as bait; this he let down upon the ground and when he thought that fish enough were assembled over it he lifted it up by very gentle and even motion, so that the fish were hardly sensible of being lifted till they were almost out of the water. By this simple method he had caught abundance of fish and I beleive it is the general way of Fishing all over this coast, as many such netts have been seen at almost every place we have been in.' (plate 70).

A few days later Cook and the scientists visited the 'Hippa' situated on the islet at the south end of Motuara, from which it was separated by a channel so narrow 'that a man might almost Jump over it' (plate 71). The precipitous sides of the island made fortification unnecessary and the defences were limited to 'a slight Palisade and one small fighting stage at one end where the rock was most accessible'. The visitors were received with 'confidence and civility' and were shown all over the village. Banks wrote, 'The people brought us several Bones of men the flesh of which they had eat, which are now become a kind of article of trade among our people who constantly ask for and purchase them for whatever trifles they have. In one part we observd a kind of wooden Cross ornamented with feathers made exactly in the form of a Crucifix cross. This engagd our attention and we were told that it was a monument for a dead man, maybe a Cenotaph as the body was not there.' Meanwhile Cook had been informed that the head of the sound did not communicate with the sea. This seemed to require further investigation.

On 22 January 1770, Cook set out in the pinnace

Plate 71. *The narrow gut between Motuara and the "Hippa Island".*

Brabejum sparsum.

Plate 72 (left). *Rewarewa or New Zealand honeysuckle* (Knightia excelsa). *This tree was described by Solander in Tolaga Bay but the specimen shown here was painted by Sydney Parkinson in 1770 at Queen Charlotte Sound.*

Plate 73 (above). Veronica floribunda. *This plant was collected by Banks and Solander at Totaranui or Queen Charlotte Sound and painted by Parkinson in 1770. It is now classified as* Hebe parviflora, *variety* arborea.

to explore the head of the inlet. After rowing 4 or 5 leagues into a fresh southerly wind, it became obvious that there was no possibility of reaching or even seeing the end of the sound that day. He wrote in his journal, 'the day already half spent we landed at noon on the SE side in order to try to get upon one of the hills to View the Inlet from thence.' Leaving Banks and Solander botanising on the shore (plates 72 and 73), Cook took a seaman and climbed the hill which seemed to offer the best prospect of obtaining a commanding view. But when he reached the top, higher hills covered with impenetrable forest still blocked his view of part of the southern horizon. Below him, however, stretched out a magnificent panorama. Even though the shoulder of Kaitapeha partially obscured his view he could still see towards the head of the

sound as far as Allports Island and the bifurcation beyond (plate 74). Looking west he could follow the intricate coastline of the Bay of Many Coves until it disappeared behind the long ridge leading up from Snake Point. He was surprised to note, when he gazed out towards the entrance of the sound, that a clear passage separated Blumine and Pickersgill Islands from the 'main' (plate 75). When he turned eastward, at his feet lay the central reaches of Tory Channel. He guessed that the swirling tide rips meant that this waterway connected directly with the sea. On lifting his eyes he saw the uninterrupted sweep of a great ocean to the east (plate 76). In his matter-of-fact way Cook recorded one of the most dramatic moments of the voyage. 'I was abundantly recompenced for the trouble I had in assending the hill, for from

Plate 74 (left). *The view south-west from Cook's Lookout. The sound stretches away past Allports Island towards its head but the junction of the Tory Channel with the main body of the sound is hidden behind a ridge of Kaitapeha.*

Plate 75 (right). *The view north-east from Cook's Lookout. The eastern coastline of the sound leads out to the entrance and the ocean beyond. The passages between Blumine Island (to the left) and Pickersgill Island beyond it and the coast are obvious from this point.*

Plate 76 (below). *The view east from Cook's Lookout. The central reaches of the Tory Channel may be seen below but its entrance to the sea is hidden by a ridge. Beyond the Strait the North Island, under a mantle of cloud, stretches away to Cape Palliser and the sweep of the eastern ocean.*

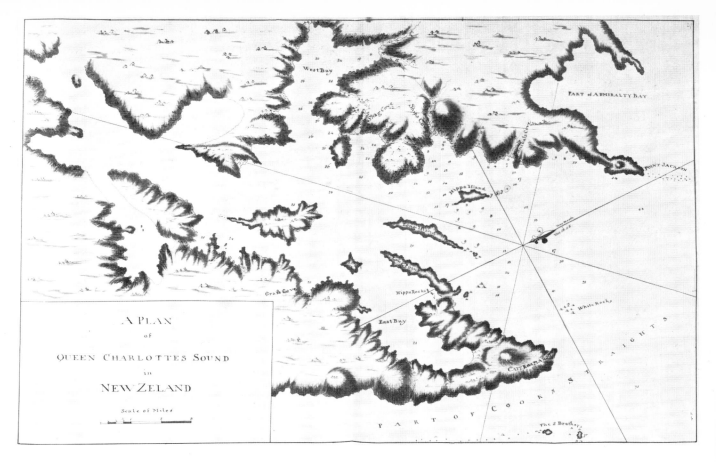

Plate 77. *The largest island towards the centre of the map is now called Blumine Island. On the peninsula to the south of it stands Kaitapeha. Dotted lines indicate that portion of the Tory Channel which Cook could not see. Cook's Lookout is the northern peak of Kaitapeha. Across the sound the dotted line representing the northern shore of the Bay of Many Coves corresponds exactly with that part which is obscured by the ridge terminating at Snake Point when it is viewed from Cook's vantage point.*

it I saw what I took to be the Eastern Sea and a strait or passage from it into the Western Sea a little to the Eastward of the entrance of the Inlet in which we now lay with the Ship.'

During this visit to Queen Charlotte Sound Cook did not penetrate again as far into the sound. On his map he drew the features beyond this point from the observations he made on this hill. What he could see he drew in confidently, but he used dotted lines to show where his vision was obscured by a hill or leading ridge (plate 77).

It is possible, by walking along the main ridge of Kaitapeha, which rises near the southern end of Arapawa Island, to see again precisely what Cook saw. There is only one vantage point on this long ridge where the visible landmarks correspond exactly with those marked on Cook's map. It is

a peak which rises to about 1,240 feet from the summit ridge of Kaitapeha about 2 miles north of its highest point. A leading spur from the south head of Umuwheke Bay ascends steeply from the sea and provides the easiest route to the summit. Though unnamed this hill dominates the central portion of Queen Charlotte Sound, and it would seem appropriate that this peak be named 'Cook's Lookout' to commemorate the discovery of his strait—the most important geographical feature of New Zealand (plate 78).

Though Cook must have realised that he had solved Tasman's riddle a slight doubt still remained. The high hills of Arapawa Island obstructed his view to the north-east—the place where the strait would be at its narrowest. He cautiously wrote, 'the main land which lies on the SE side of this inlet appeared to me to be a narrow ridge of very high hills and to form a part of the SW side of the Strait.' It is no wonder that he was in 'high spirits' as he descended the ridge to the pinnace sheltering behind the south head of Umuwheke Bay.

After they had eaten, Cook decided to make an accurate survey of the passage past Blumine and Pickersgill Islands which he had seen from his lookout. 'We set out in order to return to the Ship and in our way pass'd through and examined the Harbours, Coves &ca that lay behind the Islands above mentioned.' They passed a deserted village and saw another which was inhabited—perhaps the 'Hippa Rocks' which he marked on his chart and later visited.

On 26 January 1770, Cook took a party over to examine the western end of the strait which he had previously been unable to see. From one of the coves 'towards the head of East Bay' Cook, Banks and Solander climbed a high hill 'from which we had a full View of the passage I had before discover'd and the land on the opposite shore which appear'd to be about 4 Leagues from us.' Thus was the last lingering doubt removed, and Cook 'resolv'd after putting to sea to search this passage with the Ship'. The party built a small cairn on the top of the hill and placed some beads, small shot and musket balls under the stones in the hope of providing a lasting monument. There are several hills on this narrow spine between the

Plate 78. *The North Peak of Kaitapeha may be seen to the right with the Tory Channel beyond. A leading ridge descends to the southern point of Umuwheke Bay.*

Plate 79. *Bald Hill is a prominent feature of the narrow spine which separates East Bay from Cook Strait.*

sound and the strait which might have been climbed, but Bald Hill, which rises 840 feet above the sea, seems the most likely one and would undoubtedly have given an unobstructed view of the strait and land beyond (plate 79).

When they descended to the beach they found Tupaia and the boat's crew chatting with a group of Maoris 'in the most free and friendly way immagineable', which prompted Cook to write 'Tupia always accompanies us in every excursion we make and proves of infinate service'.

On their way back to the ship they visited the Hippa Rocks where they were well received by the Maoris. Their fortifications were situated on the largest of a chain of islets which runs out into Anatohia Bay in the shelter of a peninsula which Cook named Long Point (plate 80). The sides of the pa were precipitous and Banks complained that it was 'so steep in all parts that it was almost in danger of our necks that we climbed up to it'. Cook was astonished that so many people could crowd together into such a tiny space and Banks recorded that 'it containd maybe from 80 to 100 houses'. Though the natives were friendly they were prepared for a siege and had 'split & hanging up to dry a prodigious quantity of various sorts of small fish' which they were prepared to barter for 'such trifles as we had about us'.

Plate 80 (above). *The "Hippa Rocks" shelter within the curve of Anatohia Bay.*

Plate 81 (right). *From the top of the largest of the "Hippa Rocks", some 40 feet high, it is possible to see across the mouth of East Bay to Pickersgill Island and, far beyond it, Cook's Lookout.*

Today the Hippa Rocks are as well protected by their vertical cliffs as they ever were so that the vegetation has not been altered by wild or domestic animals (plate 81). The crown of the island strong-hold is covered with native flax (*Phormium tenax*) (plate 82) which affords some shelter for the wild celery (*Apium australe*) and prickly sow thistle or powha (*Sonchus littoralis*) (plate 83) which would once have complemented the diet of dried fish.

Cook made another reconnaissance on 29 January 1770, when he climbed a hill on the western side of the entrance to the sound, overlooking Gore Bay, and in the distance, Admiralty Bay. Here also, he erected a pile of stones on top of a piece of silver coin, some musket balls and beads, and left flying over it a part of an old pennant.

By 31 January 1770, all was ready for sea and the crew, breakfasting daily on boiled 'sellery' and 'scurvy grass' and with a plentiful supply of fresh fish, were in excellent health. But Cook, to complete his instructions before departing planned to set up marks and 'with the Consent of the Natives' to take possession of the surrounding country. The carpenter was ordered to prepare two posts with inscriptions upon them setting forth the ship's name and date. One of them was erected at the watering place at Ship Cove with the Union flag

Plate 82 (above). *Harakeke or New Zealand flax* (Phormium tenax) *painted by Nodder in 1783 from a sketch by Sydney Parkinson.*

Plate 83 (left). *Still thriving with the flax on the "Hippa Rocks" are wild celery* (Apium australe) *and powha or prickly sow-thistle* (Sonchus littoralis).

The mouth of the Harbour.   the Hippa Island. E & S.

Totaranui.

Plate 84 (above). "Totaranui." This sketch by Herman Spöring from the deck of the Endeavour shows Motuara, the "Hippa Island" and the entrance to Queen Charlotte Sound. Kapiti Island and the North Island may be seen in the distance.

Plate 85 (left). Motuara and the "Hippa Island" from Ship Cove.

upon it and the other was taken over to Motuara.

Cook, Dr Monkhouse and Tupaia then rowed across to the Maori village on the 'Hippa Island'. Here they met the old man who had welcomed them to the bay (according to Banks, Topaa by name) and, through Tupaia, Cook explained to him and to several others, that he wished to set up a mark on Motuara to indicate to any future visitors that the *Endeavour* had been there before them. At this, the Maoris 'not only gave their free consent to set it up but promised never to pull it down'. After receiving this assurance Cook distributed presents, giving to the old man a silver threepenny piece dated 1763 and some spike nails deeply engraved with 'the Kings broad Arrow', which he thought would provide durable mementoes of the occasion. The ceremony itself was described by Cook in these words. 'After I

had thus prepared the way for seting up the post we took it up to the highest part of the Island and after fixing it fast in the ground hoisted thereon the Union flag and I dignified this Inlet with the name of Queen Charlottes Sound and took formal possession of it and the adjacent lands in the name and for the use of his Majesty, we then drank Her Majestys hilth in a Bottle of wine and gave the empty bottle to the old man (who had attended us up the hill) with which he was highly pleased.'

Motuara's characteristic shape was exactly reproduced in a sketch Spöring made from the deck of the *Endeavour* (plate 84). It has two peaks, the northern one some 6 feet higher than the southern which stands 400 feet above sea level (plate 85). The Maoris must have cleared the bush from this island as it is certain that Cook would not have taken the trouble to haul the post up the hill to

Plate 86 (above). *A photograph by Russell Duncan shows the summit of Motuara in 1902.*

Plate 87 (right). *Today, trees cover the south peak of Motuara once more. Neil Begg stands beside the cairn erected in 1920 to commemorate Cook's naming of Queen Charlotte Sound and his annexation of "the adjacent lands".*

be hidden amongst the trees. However, a photograph of the site taken by Russell Duncan on 30 March 1902, shows the burnt stumps of small trees standing starkly in pasture land (plate 86). In the interval the regenerated bush had been cleared again. Now, once more, Nature is asserting herself and the grass has given way to shrubs. A few small patches of clover survive amongst the bracken and this, in turn, is being choked by a healthy growth of young five finger, wineberry, coprosma and manuka. Much of the manuka is blighted and dead but it has prepared the way for the ferns and trees. At the top of the hill the monument raised in 1920 is closely surrounded and overhung by trees more than 20 feet in height (plate 87). If the pastoralist can hold his hand for another 20 years the island will again be covered by native bush.

With Tupaia's assistance Cook directed several

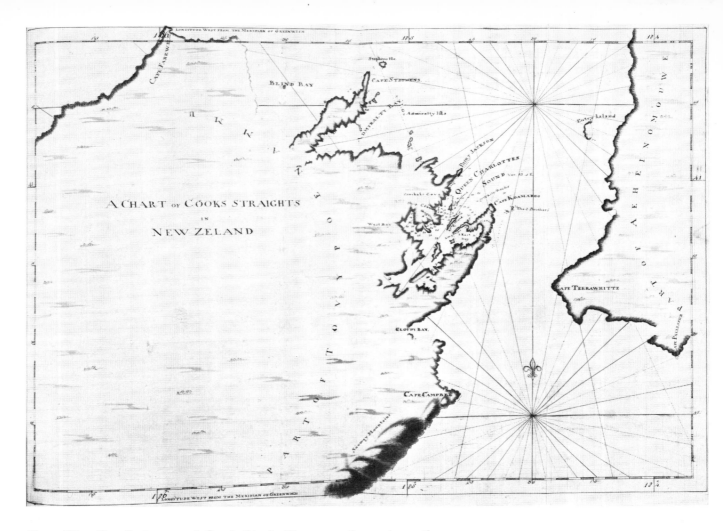

Plate 88. *The first map of Cook Strait. The soundings show the extent of the survey of Queen Charlotte Sound and the perilous route of the* Endeavour *past "The 2 Brothers".*

questions to the old man, who confirmed that there was a strait or passage to the eastern sea and that the land to the south-west of it consisted of two islands called Tovy-poenammu, which signified green talc or stone. Cook was led to believe that they could be circumnavigated in a few days—information which seemed confusing at the time. Some days later Pickersgill elicited a clearer picture of the position. From the inhabitants of a pa on the eastern side of the sound he obtained information that 'they knew but of 3 lands one of which lay to the N° which they would be 3 months in going round [Ika a Maui] another which we was upon they could go round 4 Days [Arapawa Island] and a Third lyeing SWtd of which they had but a very Imperfect knolledge and called it Towie poe namou.'

Although the ship was almost ready to sail it was not until the afternoon of 6 February 1770, that the weather permitted Cook to move out of the sound into the newly found strait—which Banks insisted on naming after its discoverer. The wind, however, dropped at the crucial moment and a fierce tide rip carried the *Endeavour* almost on to one of The Brothers Islands. The anchor, dropped in 75 fathoms, was barely able to hold her in the current which raced past at 5 knots. 'It made a very great rippling,' wrote Parkinson, 'especially near the islands, where the water, running in heaps, bears, and whirlpools, made a very great noise in its passage.' At midnight, slack water allowed the anchor to be raised with great difficulty and it was 3 hours before it reached the bows. Luckily a breeze freshened from the north and the *Endeavour*, assisted by the ebb tide, sped south through Cook Strait (plate 88).

5 Te Wai Pounamu

*Another [land] which we was upon they could go
round in 4 days and a Third lyeing SWtd of which
they had but a very Imperfect knolledge and called it
Towie poe namou.*

Richard Pickersgill

In the 4 months that the *Endeavour* had been on the coast Cook had discovered what the Maoris well knew, that Te Ika a Maui was an island and not a part of the mythical 'Southern Continent'. The strait suspected by Tasman had been proved a reality but the mysterious land of Tovey-poenammu still stretched away into the southern sea (plate 91). Cook was anxious to follow the coast and, still running before the fresh northerly breeze, he passed the southern entrance to the strait at 3 p.m. on 7 February 1770, naming it Cape Campbell. By evening the *Endeavour* was well down the coast, here dominated by 'a prodegious high mountain the summit of which was coverd with snow'— the great peak of Tapuaenuku rising 9,465 feet— then faintly lit by the setting sun.

At this moment, some of the officers, knowing that the circumnavigation of Te Ika a Maui had not been quite completed, raised the suggestion that it might be connected to the 'Southern Continent', at that point, by a narrow isthmus. Cook knew from his own observations in Queen Charlotte Sound and from the reports of the Maoris that this was most unlikely but, in order to prove this important point, the bow of the *Endeavour* was turned to the north. Next morning Cape Palliser was passed and, at 11 a.m. on 9 February 1770, Cape Turnagain was recognised 7 leagues to the north-east. 'I then called the officers upon deck and asked them if they were now satisfied that this land was an Island to which they answer'd in the affirmative and we hauled our wind to the Eastward'.

Standing once more to the south the *Endeavour* made slow progress with light and variable winds which allowed Banks to leave the ship in a boat to shoot albatrosses and petrels. The coast was obscured by a thick haze but the top of Tapuaenuku was clearly visible and, as the ship moved south along the coast on 14 February 1770, Cook drew a picture of this useful landmark towering above the Seaward Kaikouras from 6 leagues off shore (plates 89 and 90). That afternoon, while Banks was again shooting birds, four double canoes came out from the shore with 57 men aboard to investigate the strange vessel. Despite Tupaia's eloquence, however, none could be induced to come aboard. They paddled along about a stone's throw away and looked in wonder at the ship until, at dusk, they set off for 'the land like an Island [the Kaikoura Peninsula] . . . on which account' wrote Cook, 'I call'd it Lookers on'.

Next day was calm and clear. Banks, on another foray, shot six albatrosses in an hour and, at noon, Cook was still able to take a bearing of 'the Peack on the snowey Mountain', then more than 80 miles to the north. The land to the south 'seemingly detached from the Coast we were upon' was skirted at night and, at 8 a.m. on Saturday 17 February 1770, a bay was seen about 10 miles to the westward—Akaroa Harbour—near which two people were seen sitting on the top of a hill. The land had a broken and uneven surface, the tops of the hills were bare but the valleys seemed more fertile and were covered with trees. This was the first important geographical feature discovered since Cook Strait, and Cook, returning the compliment, named it Banks Island.

Early on the previous morning Lieutenant Gore was certain that he had seen land to the south-eastward. Cook, who was on deck at the time, was equally sure that it was a cloud which dissipated

Plate 89 (above). *A view of the Kaikoura coast by James Cook. Mount Tapuaenuku towers above the Seaward Kaikoura Range.*

Plate 90 (left). *Tapuaenuku and the Kaikoura Mountains from near the Clarence River in 1969.*

as the sun rose. The day's run had disclosed no land but Mr Gore was unshaken in his belief. Banks wrote in his journal, 'the Captn who resolvd that nobody should say he had left land behind unsought for orderd the ship to be steerd SE'. This course towards 'Mr Gores imaginary land' was held until the ship was 28 leagues south of Banks Peninsula and everybody was convinced that no land existed in that direction. Cook then hauled to the westward and, not realising the true significance of the information he had obtained from Topaa in Queen Charlotte Sound, expected to be able to weather the most southerly portion of the coast.

By noon next day, however, the *Endeavour* had sailed 96 miles to the west when, to everyone's surprise, land was seen extending from southeast to north-west. While the ship was tacking back and forth during the next few days, unable to make progress against a southerly wind, the haze cleared away to reveal high mountainous country far inland. Banks was delighted, 'we once more cherishd strong hopes that we had at last compleated our wishes and that this was absolutely a part of the Southern continent'. But he had to admit that his following had declined in number. 'We were now on board of two parties, one who wishd that the land in sight might, the other that it might not be a continent: myself have always been most firm for the former, tho sorry I am to say that in the ship my party is so small that I firmly beleive that there are no more heartily of it than myself and one poor midshipman, the rest begin to sigh for roast beef.'

At last the wind swung round to the north-east and Cook ran south again along the coast which

Plate 91. *Cook's map of the South Island.*

Plate 92. *Cape Saunders on the Otago Peninsula. The commanding bluff described by Cook is in the foreground, the lighthouse stands on the point behind it.*

Plate 93. *Saddle Hill from the sea. The* Endeavour *tacked close inshore and Cook drew a profile of this distinctive feature on his chart (Plate 91).*

was formed of 'pretty high hills' running parallel with the shore. Anxious to make the most of this favourable wind he crowded on too much canvas and carried away the main top gallant mast and the fore topmast studding sail boom. Repairs were soon effected and by 8 p.m. on Sunday, 24 February 1770, the *Endeavour* had reached a position 5 miles to the east of a high bluff. As darkness was falling and he was uncertain of the way the land trended Cook decided to drop anchor for the night. This point he named Cape Saunders after his old commander at the siege of Quebec (plate 92).

During the night the wind turned to the south-west and Cook had thoughts of sheltering in one of the three bays he had noticed to the north of Cape Saunders. However, the autumn was at hand and not wishing to waste time he decided to push on to the southward, 'to see as much of the coast as possible, or if this land should prove to be an Island to get round it'. And so at 4 a.m.

next morning the anchor was weighed and the *Endeavour* moved slowly to the south-west until a 'remarkable Saddle hill' (plate 93) was seen near the shore 3 or 4 leagues from Cape Saunders 'by which it may always be known when on that side of it'. The hills were of moderate height, green and woody, but there were no signs of inhabitants.

Later in the day the wind freshened to a gale accompanied by heavy rain. Cook no doubt regretted that he had not sought shelter on the coast for, battered by the storm, the *Endeavour* was forced some 150 miles off shore towards the south-east. The temperature fell but by 27 February 1770, the weather had moderated a little although Banks noted, 'no standing upon legs without the assistance of hands as yet', and a persistent heavy swell from the south-west made conditions on the ship most uncomfortable. By the beginning of March the *Endeavour* had reached the latitude of 48° south and no land could be seen in that direction, in fact, Cook was becoming doubtful of its existence, 'the SW swell still continued which makes me conjector that their is no land near in that quarter'.

Next day the wind turned to the north and the *Endeavour* stood to the west with all the sail she could carry. Several whales, seals and penguins were seen and, in the afternoon, the coast came into view. Cook sailed to within some 10 miles of the shore and saw a harbour which he named after the master, Molineux's Bay, now known as Waikawa Harbour (plate 94). No more land was seen to the south and Cook hoped he had reached the most southerly point. That night, as the ship skirted the coast, 'an immence fire on the side of a hill' was taken as an indication that this part of the country was inhabited.

The weather was thick and misty next morning,

Plate 94. *Portion of a map drawn on the* Endeavour *by Robert Molineux, the master, shows the southern part of the South Island and Stewart Island.*

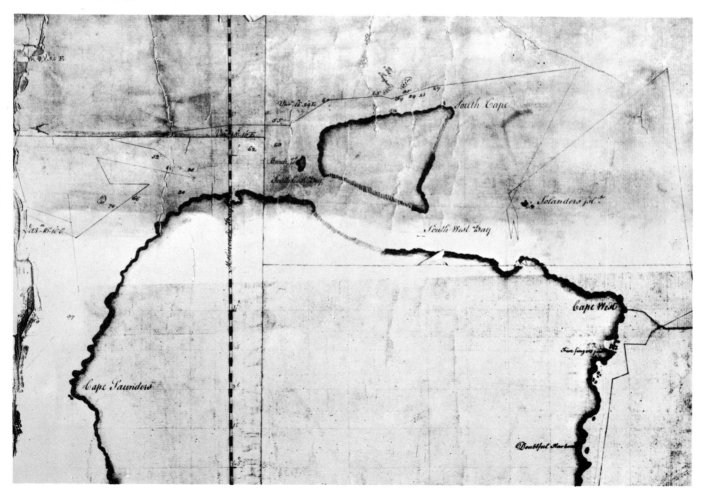

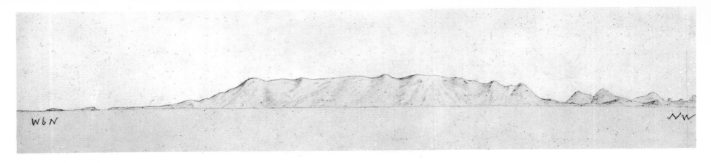

W b N   N W

Plate 95. *Sketch by Spöring of the south coast of Stewart Island.*
South Cape is on the left and the two peaks of the Fraser Mountains,
Gog and Magog, may be seen to the right of the drawing.

5 March 1770, but Cook sailed on before a south-easterly breeze. In the afternoon it cleared and a low island was seen ahead which was called Bench Island, now known by its Maori name of Ruapuke. By 5 p.m. high land was visible to the south. Again, Banks was delighted. 'Land seen as far as South so our unbeleivers are almost inclind to think that Continental measures will at last prevail.' At 8 p.m. the *Endeavour* had reached a point within 3 leagues of Ruapuke Island but Cook was still unable to decide whether there was a strait separating the two lands visible or not, 'We could not see this land join to that to the northward of us, there either being a total seperation, a deep bay or low land between them'. The wind that night was unsettled and Cook noted, 'I found the Ship in the morning considerably farther to the eastward than I expected', no doubt carried by the strength of the tide for which this region is notorious.

Calm weather persisted and the *Endeavour* could make little progress to the south 'because of a swell which took us right ahead'. But, in the evening of 8 March 1770, the wind veered to the westward and, sensing that the next day would bring the climax of the voyage, Cook held on to a south-west course all night. At daybreak, however, waves were seen breaking high on a ledge of rocks not more than $\frac{3}{4}$ mile away under the lee bow. A quick tack and a slight change of wind enabled Cook to avoid this reef and another nearer to the shore. It was a fortunate escape. Cook named these rocks The Traps 'because they lay as such to catch unwary strangers'.

The crucial day continued crisp and clear. The *Endeavour*, rising and falling with the swell, moved slowly towards the west some 12 miles off the coast which could be seen to the north more clearly than ever before. Cook described the land in sight as being of moderate height, barren aspect and as having 'very much the appearance of an Island'. Spöring made a sketch of it (plate 95). Banks was fascinated by the sunlight reflected from the polished granite cones of the Fraser Peaks 'which were amazingly full of Large Veins and patches of some mineral that shone as if it had been polishd or rather lookd as if they were realy pavd with glass'. But all on board realised that their search for the 'Southern Continent' had finished—for the meantime at least. The long hollow swell rolling up from the south-west and the vast sweep of the empty horizon made it clear that there could be no large land mass to the south for hundreds of miles. Joseph Banks noted with regret that the hills gradually declined to end in a point and gracefully acknowledged 'the total demolition of our aerial fabrick calld continent'.

All knew too that, after 19 months at sea, the *Endeavour* must soon turn north to begin the long journey home. Events seemed to demand a celebration. The birthday of a junior officer provided an excuse, the ship's dog the ingredients. Parkinson described it thus, 'being one of the inferior officers birth day, it was celebrated by a peculiar kind of festival; a dog was killed that had been bred on board; the hind quarters were roasted; and a pye was made from the fore quarters, into the crust of which they put the fat; and of the viscera they made a haggis'.

In the afternoon the wind freshened and, assisted by the set of the tide, the *Endeavour* sailed past the most southerly point of land which Cook named South Cape. He charted its position with his customary accuracy as lying in latitude 47° 19′ south, and longitude 192° 12′ west (or 167° 48′ east) from Greenwich—only 12 miles south-east of its true position—47° 17′ 30″ south latitude and 167° 32′ 30″ east longitude.

After passing the most westerly land in sight—Long or Big South Cape Island—a change in the wind allowed Cook, at last, to turn the *Endeavour* to the north. In a fresh gale the ship moved quickly along the west coast of the island, now called Stewart Island, but out of sight of the shore. At 2 a.m. next morning a steep rocky island loomed out of the darkness over the weather bow and 2 hours later land was seen ahead. Cook tacked until daylight and Banks, who was anxious to continue his studies on shore, looked eagerly towards the land (plate 96). 'We stood in with the shore which provd very high and had a most romantick appearance from the immence steepness of the hills, many of which were conical and most had their heads coverd with snow, on their sides and bottoms was however a good deal of wood, so much we could see and no more and the wind baulking us would not let us stand nearer the shore than two leagues.' Viewed from the same position nothing has changed since Banks described the scene. The snow still covers the tops of the Princess Mountains, the bush clings to the lower slopes and the long swell rolls in towards the iron-bound coast (plate 97). But no evidence of a harbour could be found and, as the wind began to blow on shore, Cook wisely stood out to sea.

Looking towards the east there seemed to be a strait. Cook wrote in his journal, 'and now we thought that the land to the southward or that we have been sailing round these two days past was an Island, because there appear'd an open Channel between the North part of that land and the south part of the other in which we thought we saw the small Island we were in with on the 6th instant, but when I came to lay this land down upon paper from the several bearings I had taken it appear'd that there was but little reason to suppose it an Id., on the Contrary I hardly have a doubt but what it joins to and makes a part of the main land. . . .' The evidence which made Cook come to this surprising decision is not clear. Most of his officers thought a strait existed between the islands and this is shown on some of the charts (plate 94).

A VIEW of the Land on the NW Side of the SW. BAY

Plate 96 (above). *Part of Cook's sketch of the southern coast of the South Island made from near the Solander Islands. On the right is The Hump, to the left of it the Princess Mountains.*

Plate 97 (right). *A view from a similar position today.*

Solander's Island

This Bark is detached from the ... at ...

Plate 98 (above). *A fine sketch by Herman Spöring of the lonely Solander Islands.*

Plate 99 (left). *The rocky shores of West Cape.*

But it must be remembered that the *Endeavour* lay some 70 miles west of Ruapuke Island and Cook could not exclude the possibility that a low peninsula might extend across the strait. The hazard of entering what might have been a deep bay before the prevailing westerly wind could not be justified, nor was time available to resolve this geographical problem which was of small consequence at that time. Furthermore, as some doubt existed, he realised that it would be improper to show a strait on his chart for this might lead subsequent voyagers into a dangerous situation. Already Cook was beginning to make plans for pursuing his search for the 'Southern Continent' elsewhere and, as the end of the season was fast approaching, he was not to be diverted easily from this prime objective of the voyage.

And so, hoping to reach his anchorage in Queen Charlotte Sound as soon as possible, Cook sailed

out of his hazardous position in South-West Bay in a squally north-west gale. He soon passed again the volcanic island which rises 1,100 feet sheer out of the sea. 'This Island I have named after Dr Solander it is nothing but a barren rock of about a Mile in circuit remar[k]ably high and lies full 5 Legues from the Main'. Herman Spöring sketched the island which Cook had named after his compatriot and a smaller one to the west of it—the Solander Islands which guard the western entrance to Foveaux Strait and were soon to become a landmark for the southern whaling fleet (plate 98).

Cook had thus cast some doubt upon the insularity of Stewart Island, a question that was to remain unsolved for more than 30 years. In 1806 the American ship *Favorite*, under Captain Jonathan Paddock, made what was probably the first passage through the strait carrying a cargo of great value—no less than 60,000 seal skins—and doubtless piloted

Cape Five Fingers.

Plate 100 (above). *Five Fingers Point drawn from the* Endeavour *by Spöring on 13 March 1770 after the ship had passed the entrance to Dusky Bay.*

Plate 101 (right). *A modern view of Five Fingers Point.*

by the man who had discovered the passage while sealing in 1804, Owen Folger Smith of Nantucket.

Heavy weather, which is almost constant in this region, forced Cook to shorten sail and it was not until the morning of 13 March 1770, that contact with the coast was regained. Inland, high mountains were visible but a thick haze obscured the coast which seemed to fade away to the north-east. About noon Cook passed the most westerly point of New Zealand naming it West Cape and fixing its position with great accuracy. His determination of latitude differs by only 40″ or 1,350 yards from that shown on the modern chart, the more remarkable as West Cape viewed from the sea is not a prominent feature being merely an inconspicuous point on a curving and rather featureless coastal shelf (plate 99).

In the afternoon the weather cleared and a promising harbour was seen into which it was

hoped to take the ship. But by 4.30 p.m. Cook found that he was still too far from the entrance to reach it before dark and, as the wind was too strong to allow a safe entry at night, the attempt to land was abandoned. This bay was named appropriately Dusky Bay and Cook, in passing, formed a good impression of its possibilities as a harbour, 'it is about 3 or 4 Miles broad at the entrance and seems to be full as deep, in it are several Islands behind which there must be shelter from all winds provided there is a sufficient depth of water'. While sailing past the northern point of the entrance Cook noticed some very remarkable peaked rocks 'standing up like the four fingers and thum of a mans hand' and from 6 miles off shore Spöring made a sketch of Point Five Fingers (plate 100), on which the sea still breaks with impressive force (plate 101).

The *Endeavour* was carried along the coast by

Plate 102. *The Southern Alps tower above the bush-clad foothills stretching to the north from Mount Cook at the right of the picture.*

a brisk breeze from the south-west and just before noon next morning, 14 March 1770, lay off the mouth of a narrow cleft in the land 'where there appear'd to be a very snug harbour form'd by an Island lying in the middle of the opening'. Four miles off shore 70 fathoms of line had failed to reach the bottom, high cliffs rose almost perpendicularly from the sea at the entrance and Pickersgill noted a similarity with the Norwegian fjords, 'the Land making high & Ragged like the coast of Noraway being craggy & Steep'. Banks had then been confined to the ship for more than 5 weeks and was most anxious to get ashore 'to examine the mineral appearances from which I had formd great hopes', but Cook refused to accept the hazard that this would have entailed. 'I saw clearly that no winds could b[l]ow there but what was either right in or right out. This is Westerly or Easterly, and it certainly would have been highly

imprudent in me to have put into a place where we could not have got out but with a wind that we have lately found does not blow one day in a month: I mention this because there were some on board who wanted me to harbour at any rate without in the least considering either the present or future concequences.' No one familiar with the entrance to Doubtful Sound would question Cook's decision but Banks, who was used to getting his way, did not forget this rebuff for many years.

Continuing along the coast before a south-west breeze the *Endeavour* sailed past Mistaken Bay—now Big Bay—with the Red Hill Range behind 'quite bare of trees or any kind of Vegetables' wrote Banks, 'and seemd to consist of a mouldering soft stone of the colour of Brick or light red ocre'. Then on past Cascades Point and Open Bay (Jackson Bay) until, by 18 March 1770, it had reached the latitude of the Fox and Franz

Josef Glaciers which Cook seems to have noticed descending into the bush from the icefields surrounding the great peaks of the Southern Alps whose tops were probably hidden in the clouds. 'The Mountains and some of the Vallies we observed this morning were wholy coverd with snow, part of which we suppos'd to have fallen in the pm and fore part of the night at the time that we had rain, and yet the weather is not cold.'

The *Endeavour* was soon following the route that Abel Tasman had taken in 1642 and conditions were much the same. Cook thought it unwise to sail too near the land 'as we had not much wind and a prodigious swell rowling in upon the Shore from the WSW'. But next day, 22 March 1770, the wind dropped and the ship drifted perilously close to the beach near Rocks Point before a light air enabled it to be manoeuvred to safety.

Cook had now sailed the whole length of Tovy-poenammu. His outstanding impression was of high mountains rising behind narrow ranges of wooded hills (plate 102). 'Close behind these hills lies the ridge of Mountains which are of a prodigious height and appear to consist of nothing but barren rocks, cover'd in many places with large patches of snow which perhaps have laid their sence the creation. No country upon earth can appear with a more ruged and barren aspect than this doth from the sea for as far inland as the eye can reach nothing is to be seen but the sumits of these Rocky mountains which seem to lay so near one another as not to admit any Vallies between them.' He thought that these mountains stretched from one end of the island to the other and on his chart he named them 'The Southern Alps'.

Equally impressive was the inhospitable lee shore on which broke continuously the long rolling southerly swell. 'Once we were very near

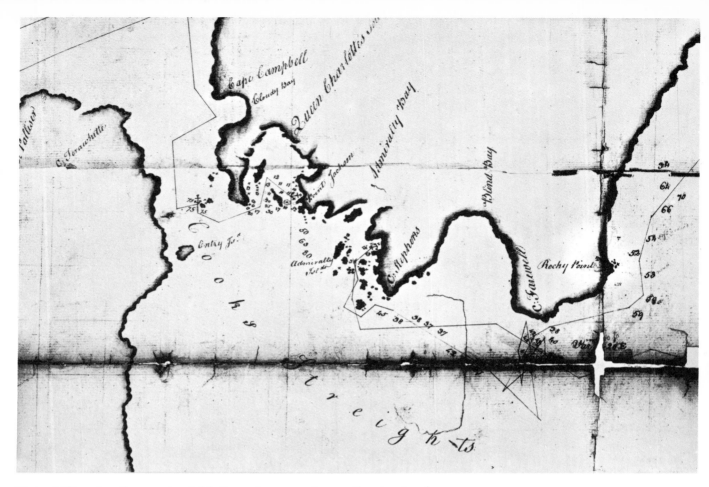

Plate 103. *Another part of Molineux's map shows the track of the* Endeavour *and where she anchored. At this time the convention of placing north at the top of the page was not always followed.*

the shore', wrote Banks, 'on which we saw that there was a most dreadfull surf, occasiond by the S and SW swell which has reignd without intermission ever since we have been upon this side of the land.'

At last, the coast turned towards the east and a course was set for Queen Charlotte Sound. Head winds were persistent however and Banks, who had been unable to land anywhere during the whole circumnavigation of the South Island wrote with some feeling, 'Light breezes but wind still at East. The sea is certainly an excellent school for patience'. But next day, 26 March 1770, Cook recognised an island he had seen to the westward from the entrance to Queen Charlotte Sound (Stephens Isle) and, rounding it, he entered Abel Tasmans Reede (plate 103) in 'hazey misty weather with drizling rain'. At 6 p.m. the ship was anchored in 11 fathoms of water in the shelter of D'Urville

Island, just south of Old Man's Point (plate 104).

The time had come to leave New Zealand. Early next morning the *Endeavour* was moved to a convenient berth and wood and water began to come aboard. Fortunately fish were plentiful. Tupaia and his boy soon caught a boat-load and one day 90 fish were caught out of the cabin windows alone. Banks and Solander were not slow to go ashore but were disappointed at not being able to find one new plant. By 30 March 1770, the weather had cleared and Banks decided to make another search for plants. 'I resolvd to climb some hill in hopes of meeting some plants in the upper regions as none had been found in the lower. I did with great dificulty, walking for more than a mile in fern higher than my head; success however answerd my wishes and I got 3 plants which we had not before seen.' One of these plants proved to be *Celmisia gracilenta*, a species of mountain

Plate 104. *An aerial view of Admiralty Bay looking north along the eastern coast of D'Urville Island. The Endeavour anchored on the near side of Old Man's Point in the left foreground. Beyond is Tasman's anchorage inside the Rangitoto Islands with Stephens Island in the distance.*

Plate 105. *Sydney Parkinson's unfinished sketch of* Celmisia gracilenta (above) *was made in Admiralty Bay in 1770. F. P. Nodder completed the painting* (right) *in 1779.*

Plate 106. *Cook climbed a hill on D'Urville Peninsula (foreground) and saw the passage through French Pass to the south.*

daisy for which the alpine slopes of the New Zealand peaks were later to become famous. Parkinson's unfinished drawing of this plant may be seen in plate 105.

Meanwhile Cook, making the most of his last chance of investigating the coast, set off in the pinnace 'in order to examine the Bay and to explore as much of it as the little time I had would admit'. After rowing south along the coast for about 5 miles he landed and climbed a hill (plate 106). From it he was able to see the arm of the bay extending some 15 miles towards the south-west, although he could not discern its head. No doubt he was looking into French Pass where D'Urville narrowly averted shipwreck in 1827. Cook searched for signs of the natives but discovered nothing other than some old huts, long since deserted.

On his return to the *Endeavour* Cook found that preparations for departure had been completed and it was necessary to decide 'the Most Eligible way of returning home'. In the evening a consultation with the officers was held. Cook wished to return by way of Cape Horn which would have allowed a further search for the 'Southern Continent', but it was agreed that the condition of the ship would not stand such a journey in the winter months. For the same reason a direct return by way of the Cape of Good Hope was rejected. Instead, it was resolved to sail by way of the East Indies and the Cape after having followed northwards the eastern coast of New Holland.

No time was lost and at daybreak next morning, 31 March 1770, the *Endeavour* sailed from Admiralty Bay on the long journey home.

6 The Master Plan

The most feasable Method of making further discoveries
in the South Sea is to enter it by way of New Zeland

James Cook

As Cape Farewell dropped below the horizon on 1 April 1770 the main purpose of the voyage was complete. Cook had sailed right round 'the Land discover'd by Tasman and now called New Zeland' and had found no evidence of the 'Southern Continent'. He had carefully observed the 'Latitude and Longitude in which that Land is situated' and he had taken possession of 'Convenient Situations' in the name of the King of Great Britain. But the voyage was by no means over yet.

Cook could not know of the drama which awaited him amongst the treacherous coral reefs off the Australian coast. Much less could he foresee the tragedy of the disease ridden tropics where malaria and dysentery exacted a merciless toll of the ship's company and turned the *Endeavour* into a floating hospital. But despite the vicissitudes of the homeward voyage the unsolved problem of the 'Southern Continent' was never far from his thoughts. Since rounding South Cape on Stewart Island in March 1770, Cook had wondered how best to solve this question and, before the *Endeavour* had, at last, reached the Thames on 13 July 1771, he had formulated a plan for completing 'the discoveries in the South Sea'. This plan was added as a postscript to his encyclopaedic journal which, together with his charts, views and bundles of 'curiosities', formed a contribution, the like of which the Admiralty had never received before.

Once ashore Cook gave further thought to his proposal. He examined the map of the Pacific Ocean and the Southern Hemisphere and marked on it the tracks of the ships of those who had preceded him—Tasman, Wallis and Bougainville. He also drew in the course the *Endeavour* had taken. There remained some areas in the higher latitudes which were uncharted and Cook was anxious to continue his explorations in these unknown seas. He marked, with a yellow crayon, a route which avoided the course of previous navigators, and which would take him to the last unexplored areas of the Pacific Ocean. He wrote down his suggestions and presented them, with his map, to the Right Honourable the Earl of Sandwich, First Commissioner of the Board of Admiralty on 6 February 1772 (plates 107 and 108).

His experiences during the first voyage helped considerably in his planning for the second. He and his predecessors in the Pacific had established the pattern of the prevailing winds (plate 109). The warm trade winds flowed to the west in the tropical and subtropical seas while the 'roaring forties' roistered eastwards in the higher latitudes to the south. He had also become aware of the marked seasonal variations. His efforts to probe the mysteries of the Antarctic seas would have to be undertaken during the brief weeks of January and February when the southern summer was at its height. Other voyages of exploration could be made to the warmer climates of the Central Pacific during the winter months from June to November.

Perhaps most important of all, he had discovered a safe harbour in Queen Charlotte Sound which would make an admirable forward base. Here he had established good relations with the Maoris and there were plentiful supplies of food, wood and fresh water. It was a suitable starting point for a voyage to the south, yet was within easy striking range of the islands of the Pacific (plate 110).

Cook also drew the attention of the Admiralty to the unexplored areas of the South Atlantic Ocean.

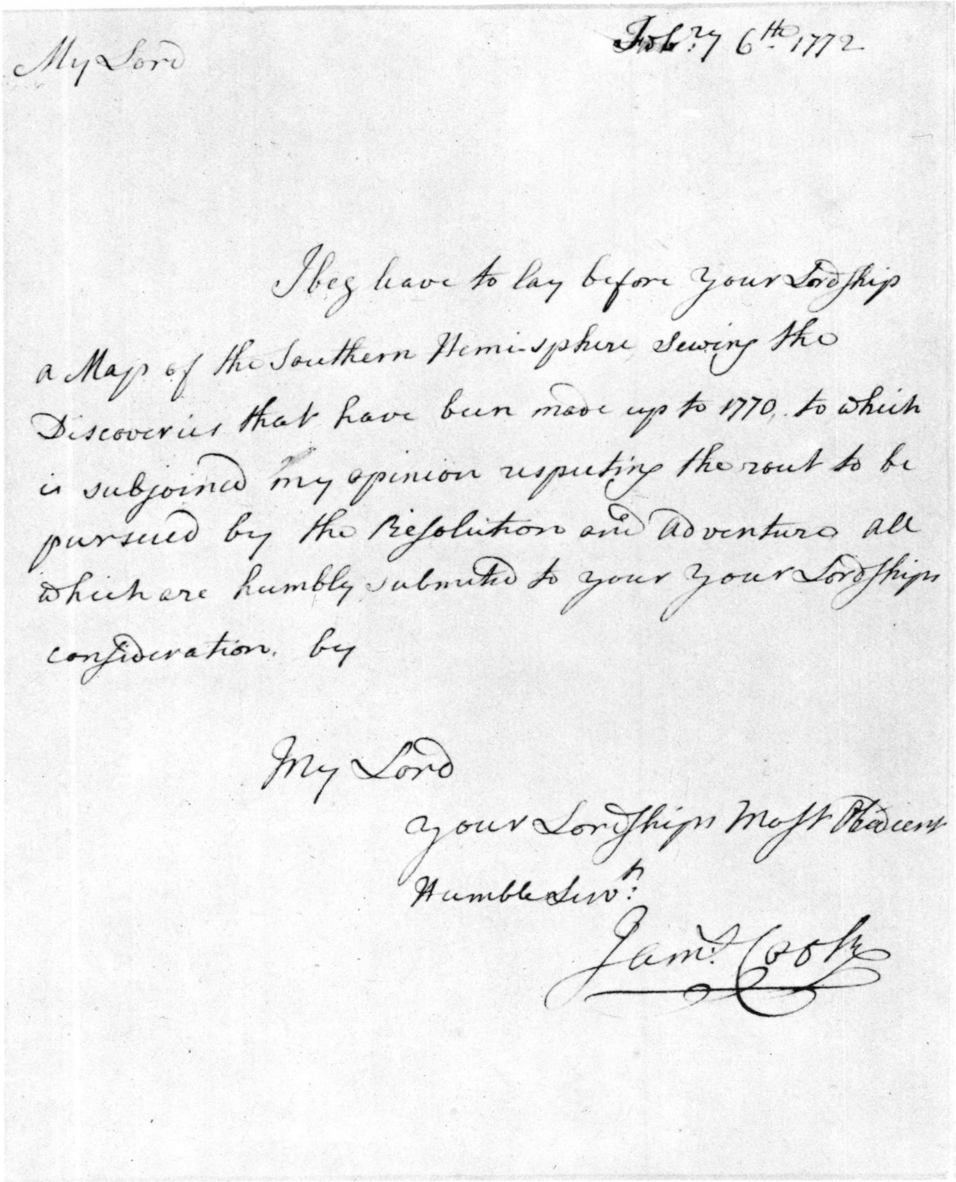

My Lord

Feb 6th 1772

I beg leave to lay before your Lordship a Map of the Southern Hemisphere shewing the Discoveries that have been made up to 1770, to which is subjoined my opinion respecting the rout to be pursued by the Resolution and Adventure all which are humbly submitted to your your Lordships consideration. by

My Lord

Your Lordships Most Obedient Humble Servt.

Jams Cook

Plate 107. *Cook's letter to the Earl of Sandwich.*

'Therefore to make new discoveries the Navigator must Traverse or Circumnavigate the Globe in a higher parallel than has hitherto been done, and this will be best accomplished by an Easterly Course on account of the prevailing westerly winds in all high Latitudes.' To illustrate his plan he used his map—'The Yellow line on the Map shews the track I would propose the Ships to make, Supposeing no land to intervene, for if land is discovered the track will be altered according to the directing of the land, but the general rout must be pursued otherwise some part of the Southern Ocean will remain unexplored.'

Nor were practical considerations forgotten and Cook provided the Admiralty with the following suggestions. 'I give it as my opinion that the most feasable Method of making further discoveries in the South Sea is to enter it by the way of New Zeland, first touching and refreshing at the Cape of Good Hope, from thence proceed to the Southward of New Holland for Queen Charlottes Sound where again refresh Wood and Water, takeing care to be ready to leave that place by the latter end of September or beginning of October at farthest, when you would have the whole summer before you and after geting through the Straight might, with the prevailing Westerly winds, run to the Eastward in as high a Latitude as you please. . .'

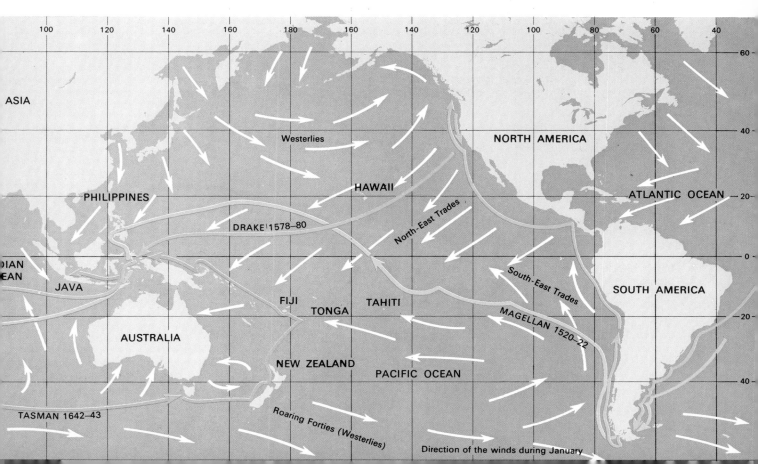

Plate 108 (right). *The master plan. Cook marked in yellow crayon his suggested route to the unexplored regions of the Pacific Ocean.*

Plate 109 (below). *A map showing the prevailing winds of the Pacific Ocean and how they determined the course of some of the earlier navigators.*

A MAP OF THE SOUTHERN-HEMISPHERE

Shewing the Discoveries made in the Southern Ocean up to 1770

AFRICA
Cape of Good Hope
Madagascar
SOUTH AMERICA
NEW ZEALAND
NEW HOLLAND

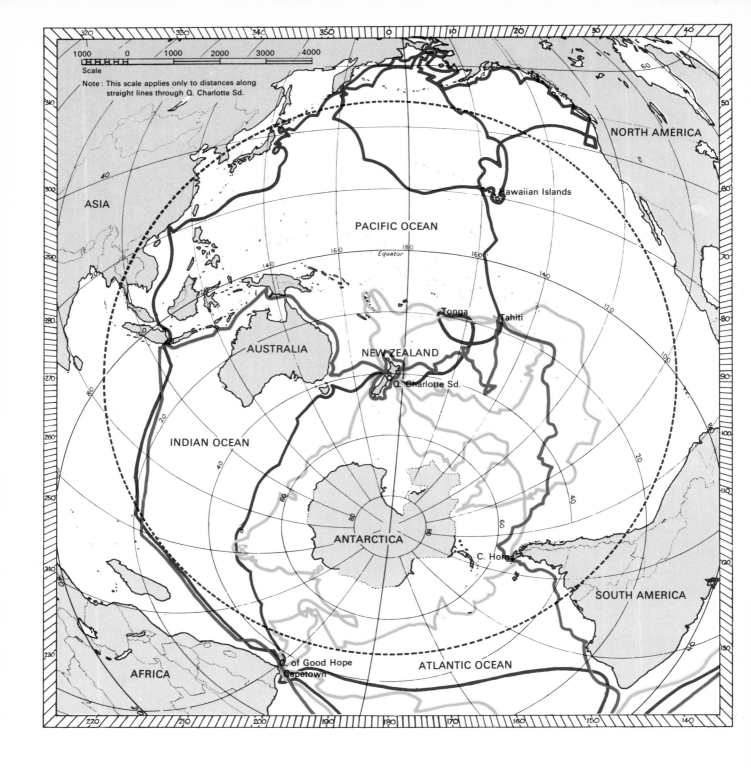

Plate 110. *The extent of the oceanic hemisphere and the central position of Queen Charlotte Sound are shown on this map. It has been drawn on an oblique equidistant azimuthal projection which results in every great circle through Queen Charlotte Sound being 'unrolled' into a straight line in the projection plane, with its correct length and initial direction preserved. It is thus possible to measure, with the scale provided, distances from Queen Charlotte Sound, and, in addition,* *to read off from the marginal angular scale the azimuths or bearings, from this centre, of any of the features charted by Cook on his voyages of exploration in the Pacific Ocean and Antarctic Seas.*

Having found out the physical advantages of his base at Ship Cove, Cook soon recognised the special value of its geographical position for continuing his search for the 'Southern Continent', as outlined in his master plan for making 'new discoveries'.

THE SECOND VOYAGE
7 Towards New Zealand

Thus we went on in the most severe frost, wet and
cold, running the gauntlet every day among the Ice
accompanied by nothing but whales and a few
melancholly birds

Tobias Furneaux

The Lords of the Admiralty were quick to see the simplicity and strength of Cook's proposals and did everything possible to expedite the plan. The magnitude of the projected voyage, and no doubt the dangers of the coral seas which so nearly brought the *Endeavour's* journey to an untimely end, caused everyone to agree that this time there should be two vessels sailing in consort. The Admiralty purchased the *Marquis of Granby*, 462 tons, and the *Marquis of Rockingham*, 340 tons, both, like the *Endeavour*, built at the Fishburn shipyards at Whitby. They were at first renamed the *Drake* and *Raleigh*, but as some thought that these names might offend the susceptibilities of the

Spanish they were finally christened the *Resolution* and *Adventure*. The ships were taken to Deptford and Woolwich to be fitted out for the voyage with all possible speed.

It was not without some difficulty that the crew was selected. Clerke, Pickersgill and Edgcumbe of the marines, all officers who had sailed with the *Endeavour* returned to join the new expedition. In addition, 13 seamen and 1 marine offered their services again. Captain Tobias Furneaux (plate 112), who had visited Tahiti with Wallis, was appointed to the *Adventure* as commander with a complement of 80 men. In the *Resolution* Cook, now promoted to commander, took with him Robert

Plate 111. *The routes taken by the* Resolution *and* Adventure *on their voyages to New Zealand.*

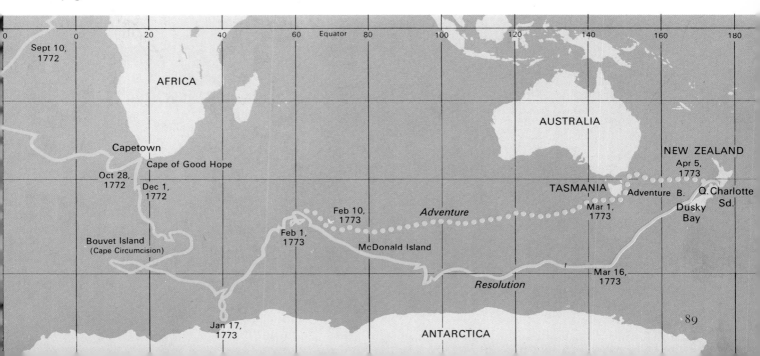

Plate 112. *Captain Tobias Furneaux. Portrait painted by James Northcote in 1776.*

Palliser Cooper as first lieutenant, Charles Clerke and Richard Pickersgill as lieutenants, John Edgcumbe as lieutenant of the marines and Joseph Gilbert as master. The surgeon was James Patten and one of his assistants was a young Scottish doctor with wide interests in natural history, William Anderson. The midshipmen, boys of 13 to 15 years of age, included John Elliott, who wrote lively and informative memoirs, and George Vancouver who was later to lead another voyage of exploration to the Pacific. All in all there were 110 men under Cook's command in the *Resolution*.

The date of departure was set for March 1772, but there were delays in the refitting of the ships. One of the most serious centred around Mr Joseph Banks. Both Banks and Cook, as the result of the *Endeavour's* successful voyage, had become famous men. Cook avoided the limelight and went about his business and family life without ostentation. Banks, however, bathed in the glory of his accomplishments with obvious pleasure. He walked with the king and with ministers of state and recounted his stories of adventure and discovery.

The *Endeavour*, her captain and crew were merely a vehicle for his explorations. Naturally he would accompany Cook on his next expedition. To implement this desire he selected some scientists and artists to accompany him and requested the Admiralty to provide additional accommodation for his staff and equipment. Accordingly, the great cabin of the *Resolution* was enlarged and a superstructure erected on the deck.

But it was not to be. On sailing from Gravesend it was found that the ship was so top heavy as to be actively dangerous. Clerke wrote—'By God, I'll go to sea in a grog-tub, if required, or in the *Resolution* as soon as you please, but must say I think her by far the most unsafe ship I ever saw or heard of.' Cook agreed and, with the approval of the Admiralty, the *Resolution* was taken to Sheerness for the removal of the offending structure. This according to John Elliott, reduced Mr Banks to anger and despair. 'Mr Banks came to Sheerness and when he saw the ship, and the Alterations that were made, He swore and stamp'd upon the Warfe, like a Mad Man; and instantly order'd his servants, and all his things out of the Ship.' Indeed, Banks and his entourage withdrew from the expedition and satisfied themselves with a trip to Iceland.

Into the breach strode Johann Reinhold Forster, born in Polish Prussia in 1729, a scientist of wide interests, with his brilliant son George who, though not yet 18 years of age, was already an accomplished linguist, a competent ornithologist and a gifted artist (plate 113). The elder Forster had, at least to English eyes, some of the less attractive Teutonic characteristics of arrogance and intolerance. His cantankerous nature, however, was balanced by the qualities of thoroughness and industry. The Forsters were well aware of their deficiencies in botanical knowledge and by a fortunate chance met a young Swedish botanist, Dr Anders Sparrman, when the *Resolution* reached the Cape of Good Hope. Though never regarded as generous, Johann Forster prevailed on Sparrman to join the expedition and paid his expenses and a small stipend. The Forsters, father and son, and Anders Sparrman had the makings of a first-class scientific team.

There was important navigational research to do and William Wales, an astronomer, was appointed to accompany Cook on the *Resolution*, while his colleague, William Bayly, was posted to the *Adventure*. One of their tasks was to check the accuracy of the 'Watch-machines' for determining longitude. They were instructed by the Board of Longitude to do this by the 'lunar' method devised by Dr Nevil Maskelyne in 1761 which depended upon the measurement with a sextant of the angular distance of the moon from the sun and seven selected stars (plate 114). This was an accurate method, as Green and Cook had proved on the *Endeavour* voyage, but the computation took some 4 hours even with the help of tables from *The Nautical Almanac*, first published in 1766 by Maskelyne, with the help of Wales and Bayly. Longitude is linked with the rotation of the earth and therefore time, but pendulum clocks were useless at sea. In 1714 the Board of Longitude offered a prize of £20,000 for the discovery of a method of finding longitude to within 30 miles. John Harrison devoted a lifetime of careful work to this problem and his fourth timepiece was successfully tested in 1761–2. The Board of Longitude reluctantly granted half the prize on condition that he surrendered all his clocks. A skilled watchmaker, Larcum Kendall, made an exact copy of Harrison's fourth timekeeper, and it was this beautiful instrument, just over 5 inches in diameter, which was taken on the voyage (plate 115), together with three other watches made by John Arnold.

When Banks departed from the scene he also removed John Zoffany, who was to have been the expedition's artist. Instead William Hodges was appointed. He was a young man with a pleasing nature and a considerable talent for land and seascapes. His pictures of the ice in the limitless Antarctic waters, and his mastery of the light and brilliance of the warmer seas and the tropical skies, are still a delight.

The projected date of departure came and went. Still the ships were not ready and the season was slipping away. Captain Cook had supervised the fitting out and his examination found it faultless, once the offending top hamper had been removed. He checked the *Resolution's* equipment and watched over the provisioning processes. He knew that this was of critical importance, for his men would not survive on the ordinary fare of salt meat and ship's biscuit. Innovations were essential, 'Some alterations were adopted in the species of provision usually made use of in the navy. . . . We had besides many extra articles such as malt, sour krout, salted cabbage, portable broth, saloup, mustard, marmalade of carrots, and inspissated

Plate 113. *Johann and George Forster from a painting by T. F. Rigau.*

juice of wort and beer. Some of these articles had before been found to be highly antiscorbutic; and others were now sent out on trial, or by way of experiment.'

Although the expedition was primarily one of exploration, it was well-equipped to undertake applied research in navigation and medicine and was ready to collect, classify and record discoveries in the field of natural history. James Cook, at the age of 44 years, was at the peak of his powers, and well prepared to lead an expedition of such magnitude and scope as had never been attempted before.

At last preparations were complete and the *Resolution* and *Adventure* left Plymouth Sound at 6 a.m. on Monday, 13 July 1772. To mark their departure from England Francis Holman, a well-known naval artist, had painted a picture of the ships some days previously (plate 116) and they had been thoroughly farewelled by Lord Sandwich and Captain Palliser, who had both done so much for the expedition.

Though their start had been delayed the ships

Plate 114 (above). *Sextant used by Cook on the* Endeavour. *Many years ago this sextant was purchased from Captain J. Patterson of Peterhead, Aberdeenshire, Scotland, the grandson of one of the* Endeavour's *crew, by Professor James Park, who presented it to the McNab Collection of the Dunedin Public Library, in 1936.*

Plate 115 (left). *The "Watch-machine", made by Larcum Kendall in 1767–69, which accompanied Cook on his second and third voyages. It is now in the National Maritime Museum at Greenwich.*

Plate 116 (above). *Before the* Resolution *and* Adventure *left England, Francis Holman, a famous naval artist, painted this picture. To the right the ships are shown broadside on, to the left a stern view is presented. The figurehead of the* Resolution *may be clearly seen.*

Plate 117 (right). *The figurehead of the* Resolution—*a hound in full cry. It is now in the Dominion Museum in Wellington, and is the only remaining part of the ship.*

made good time to Cape Town, and on Sunday, 30 October 1772, dropped anchor in Table Bay after 109 days at sea, which included a stop at Madeira for wine and at the Canary Isles for water. Already the experimental brews of beer, the sauerkraut and the salted cabbage, together with good hygiene of the ship and the enforced cleanliness of the crew were proving themselves. At Cape Town, Cook wrote—'At this time we have not one man on the Sick list, the People in general have injoy'd a good state of health ever since we left England.' For those of Cook's crew who objected to the strange foods the lesson was reinforced by the arrival at Cape Town of two Dutch ships, 4 or 5 months out of Europe, '. . . in which one lost by the Scurvy & other putrid diseases 150 Men, and the other 41, and sent on their arrival great numbers to the Hospital, in very dreadfull circumstances.'

Cook also reported on his navigational researches. 'Mr Kendalls Watch thus far has been found to answer beyond all expection.'

The expedition was considerably behind schedule and should have left Cape Town late in October. There were the inevitable delays in provisioning, however, and 3 weeks went by. The men benefited

Plate 118. *The ships at anchor in Table Bay. William Hodges painted this picture in November 1772.*

by fresh food and 'as much greens as they could eat'. Gilbert charted the bay and Hodges 'employed himself in Drawing a View of the Town and Port adjacent in Oyle Colours' (plate 118). The Forsters met and recruited Sparrman, and Cook himself picked up some port-side gossip about recent voyages of exploration. He also wrote to his old friend and master John Walker of Whitby—'You must have heard of the Clamour raised against the Resolution before I left England. I can assure you I never set foot in a finer Ship.'

At 3 p.m. on Monday, 22 November 1772, the *Resolution* and the *Adventure* weighed anchor and, leaving civilisation behind, headed out into the unknown seas.

Cook's first task was to find Cape Circumcision, discovered and named by Lozier Bouvet in 1739. The directions given were accurate as to latitude but, as always, sadly astray in longitude. They were inadequate for the finding of such a minute dot in a thousand miles of ocean and the ships sailed to the east of its true position. Next came the first foray into the far south. The pack ice and the icebergs, the fogs and the gales together with the intense, pervading cold made the voyage a nightmare. On 4 January 1773, Cook wrote in his journal—'strong gales attended with a thick Fogg Sleet and Snow, all the Rigging covered with Ice and the air excessive cold, the Crew however stand it tolerable well, each being cloathed with a fearnought Jacket, a pair of Trowsers of the same and a large Cap made of Canvas & Baize, these together with an additional glass of Brandy every Morning enables them to bear the Cold without Flinshing.' By 17 January 1773, the ships had reached the incredible position of 67° 15′ South, and had become the first to penetrate the Antarctic Circle. 'From the mast head I could see nothing to the Southward but Ice, in the Whole extent from East to WSW without the least appearance of any partition. . . .' They had reached a position only 75 miles north of Enderby Land, part of the Antarctic continent. 'I did not think it was consistant with the safty of the Sloops or any ways prudent for me to persevere in going farther to the South as the summer was already half spent. . . .' They left the whales, the petrels and the penguins to their inhospitable icefields and turned north (plate 119).

By early February the ships had returned north to a latitude of about 48° south, and were looking for an island lately described by the French. Charles Clerke wrote, 'We've been for these 6 or 7 days past cruizing for the Land the Frenchman gave intelligence of at the Cape of Good Hope—if my friend Monsieur found any Land, he's been confoundedly out in the Latitude & Longitude of it, for we've search'd the spot he represented it in and its Environs too pretty narrowly and the devil an Inch of Land is there.' The presence of birds and penguins, however, made Cook suspect that land was near and, in fact, they sailed between Kerguelen and McDonald Islands.

The ships were now in the path of the westerlies and they ran the easting down until they became separated in a gale on 8 February 1773. The *Resolution* searched for the *Adventure* for 3 days and then ran on before the winds again. Furneaux made his way to warmer waters and a planned rendezvous with Cook at Queen Charlotte Sound. The officers of the *Resolution* also looked longingly towards the north. Cook recorded that there were 'still some hopes of meeting with land and various were the oppinions among the officers of its situation. Some said we should find it to East others to the North, but it was remarkable that not one gave it as his opinion that any was to be found to the South which served to convince me that they had no inclination to proceed any farther that way. I however was resolved to get as far to the South as I conveniently could . . .'

By 17 February 1773, the *Resolution* was again in the ice. Hodges painted some lonely seascapes amongst the ice islands (plate 120) and showed the boat crews bringing in large pieces to melt for drinking water. Wales was fascinated by the brilliance of the aurora—the southern lights or aurora australis—and Pickersgill thought it 'superior to the Aurora Borealis, for the Colours are finer and the flashes more quick and beautifull'. The icebergs in the summer months were in a dangerous condition and one 'turned nearly bottom up while we were near it' and another split in half with a thunderous roar. By 23 February 1773, the *Resolution* had reached the position of 61° 52′ south at about 95° east of Greenwich and again Cook was only a stone's throw from the Antarctic continent—this time north of Queen Mary Land. The number and size of the icebergs increased and Cook was aware of both their beauty and their danger. 'A view . . . at once fills the mind with admiration and horror, the first is occasioned by the beautifullniss of the Picture and the latter by

Plate 119 (above). *The broad-billed prion or parara (Pachyptila vittata vittata), painted by George Forster, in the Southern Ocean.*

Plate 120 (right). *The* Resolution *and* Adventure *thread their way through the "Ice Islands". Painting by William Hodges.*

Plate 121. *The entrance to Dusky Bay, painted by William Hodges, on 26 March 1773.*

the danger attending it, for was a ship to fall aboard one of these large pieces of ice she would be dashed to pieces in a moment.'

Gales drove the ship eastwards until 17 March 1773, when Cook made the decision to turn north in order to find some rest for his hard-pressed crew. 'If the reader of this Journal desires to know my reasons for taking the resolution just mentioned I desire he will only consider that after crusing four months in these high Latitudes it must be natural for me to wish to injoy some short repose in a harbour where I can procure some refreshments for my people of which they begin to stand in need of, to this point too great attention could not be paid as the Voyage is but in its infancy.' He wasted no time in moving north and on 19 March 1773, wrote, 'I shaped my Course for New Zealand and being under no apprehensions of meeting with any danger I was not backward in carrying sail as well by night as day, having the advantage of a very strong gale. . . .' The *Resolution* had sailed for 123 days in the most arduous conditions

and through uncharted seas. In that time she had covered about 10,980 nautical miles.

At 10 a.m. on Friday, 25 March 1773, the mountains of southern New Zealand were sighted from the masthead and the *Resolution* rapidly closed with the shore until 4.30 p.m. when visibility deteriorated. 'Fearing to run into a place in thick weather we were utter strangers to, I tacked in 25 fm water and stood out to sea.' There had just been time to see 'a White clift which is on one of the Islands which lies about the middle of the Mouth of the Bay'. Cook's prudence, as well as his courage, must have saved his ship and his crew on many occasions. It is as well that he turned away, for dead ahead lay Table Rock and Balleny Reef which make the entry to Chalky Inlet hazardous except in the clearest weather. The ship ran north past West Cape next morning until Cook recognised Point Five Fingers. Then, with all sail set he steered for the entrance of Dusky Bay in which he had decided to seek rest and refreshment.

8 Dusky Bay

*For every Island, of which there are almost an infinite
number, is a mountain; and the Country a heap of
Mountains piled one upon another, untill you lose their
Tops in the Clouds*

William Wales

As the *Resolution* opened Dusky Bay, William Hodges was busy making a wash drawing of the entrance and its surrounding features. It was standard practice to make rapid topographical sketches of the coast and harbours, but in this one Hodges invested something of his artistry. He finished it in delicate colour and added a glowing sky (plate 121). The majestic mountains, sliced steeply by glacial action, towered above the little ship, and the water below was too deep for soundings (plate 122). Though Cook had found a depth of 44 fathoms outside the bay, where the ancient glaciers had deposited the moraine, inside he could find no bottom. But it was too late to turn back and he began to thread his way carefully between the islands in search of an anchorage. George Forster described the scene. 'The weather was delightfully fair, and genially warm, when compared to what we had lately experienced; and we glided along by insensible degrees, wafted by light airs, past numerous rocky islands, each of which was covered with wood and shrubberies, where numerous evergreens were sweetly contrasted and mingled with the various shades of autumnal yellow. Flocks of aquatic birds enlivened the rocky shores, and the whole country resounded with the wild notes of the feathered tribe.' In this idyllic setting two boats were lowered to prospect

Plate 122. *The entrance to Dusky Sound today.*

for an anchorage. This they found at the easterly point of Anchor Island and, at 3 p.m. on Saturday, 26 March 1773, the *Resolution* was anchored in 50 fathoms of water 'so near the shore as to reach it with a hawser'.

Though the ship was protected from the westerly winds and sheltered from the great ocean swell Cook was worried about the safety of his anchorage. He, himself, took a boat north to discover a landlocked harbour under some towering cliffs which he named Facile Harbour. Richard Pickersgill explored to the south and returned to the ship with a description of a haven which seemed more suitable. Next morning at 9 a.m. on Sunday, 27 March 1773, Cook got his ship under sail and with a south-west breeze worked his way past Indian Island through a narrow channel into the quiet waters of Pickersgill Harbour (plate 123). The boats were lowered and the *Resolution* was hauled, stern first, into a small cove and moored to the trees, in 5 fathoms of water. There was fresh water in a clear stream which flowed into the harbour less than 100 yards from the ship. Fish were in plenty and wildfowl abounded. Cook's desire 'to injoy some short

repose in a harbour where I can procure some refreshments for my people' had been attained. Dusky Bay also satisfied his explorer's instinct. He might have sailed directly to his rendezvous with Furneaux in Queen Charlotte Sound but 'the Discovery of a good Port in the Southern part of this Country and to find out its produce were objects more intresting'.

There was one subject which was uppermost in Cook's mind. It is hard for us today to understand what a tremendous contribution Cook had made, in his southern voyage, to the defeat of scurvy. He, himself, was amazed and delighted that only one man had symptoms of scurvy though they had been over 4 months at sea 'without once having sight of land'.

The human body can store vitamin C for about 3 months. If the body reserves of this vitamin are not replenished during this period, by fruit or green vegetables, scurvy develops. It was first described during the Crusades and was common at that time both in the invading armies and the people of besieged cities. When sailors and explorers began to make long voyages away from land, for instance, that made from Portugal to India and

treatise on the disease, its cure and prevention by the use of orange juice. But, as always in preventive medicine, knowledge was not quickly translated into action. It proved difficult to change the habits of the Navy and the men who served in its ships. James Cook had the intelligence to see the importance of Lind's work and had the driving force to ensure that this knowledge was applied. He well knew that scurvy posed the greatest single threat to the success of his voyage.

Seen in this light it is easy to understand the exhilaration evident in Cook's journal at the end of his great journey to Dusky Sound. He mentioned the health of his crew even when the *Resolution* was still in the hazardous anchorage under Anchor Point. His first act was to send his officers out to secure a seal—'one of which they killed which afforded us a fresh Meal'. He also ordered out a boat which caught a great quantity of fresh fish for his men. The next day, as soon as the ship was safely moored in Pickersgill Harbour he sat down and wrote a letter to Captain Furneaux. 'Whereas scurvey grass, sellery, and other vegitables are to be found in most uncultivated countries, especially in New Zealand, and when boil'd with wheat or oatmeal, with a proper quantity of portable broth, makes a very wholesome and nourishing diet, and has been found to be of great use against all scorbutick complaints . . . you are therefore hereby required and directed, whenever vegitables are to be got, to cause a sufficient quantity to be boil'd . . . every morning for breakfast for the company of his Majesty's sloop under your command. . . . Given under my hand, on board his Majesty's sloop Resolution, in Dusky Bay, this 28th day of March 1773.   J. Cook.'

Cook's enthusiasm bubbled out in this interminable sentence without thought as to how the missive would be delivered to Captain Furneaux. To him the defeat of scurvy was a greater satisfaction than his geographical discoveries. The secret lay not only in the vitamin but also in the commander who saw to it that the antiscorbutic foods were eaten. This was not achieved without a struggle and Cook explained—'To interduce any New article of food among Seamen, let it be ever so much for their good, requires both the example and Authority of a Commander, without both of which, it will be droped before the People are Sencible of the benifits resulting from it; was it necessary, I could name fifty instances in support of this remark. Many of my People, officers as

back by Vasco da Gama between 1497 and 1499, scurvy became a disease of seafaring men and was called 'sea scurvy'. From the fifteenth century to the end of the eighteenth century scurvy killed more seamen than wars and shipwreck combined. It would appear with unfailing regularity when the ship was 3 months out of port and would spread through the crew until all were affected and many were dead. It is not too much to say that lengthy exploration was limited, or made impossible, for 500 years by the ravages of sea scurvy.

The Royal Navy recognised the severity of the problem when Lord Anson led an expedition of six ships round the world in 1740–44. Three-quarters of his men, some 1,200 in all, succumbed to the disease before the remnants of his crippled fleet limped back to England. The Reverend Richard Walter, Chaplain to Anson's flagship *Centurion* described the weakness, the discoloured skin, the putrid gums and the swollen legs. Many of the men fell dead on the slightest exertion.

But in 1753 James Lind (plate 124), a Scottish naval surgeon, gave hope of a solution to the problem. From a study of history, and from his own experience on HMS *Salisbury*, he wrote a

well as seamen, at first, disliked Celery, Scurvy grass &ca being boiled in the Pease & Wheat and some refused to eat it, but as this had no effect on my conduct, this obstinate kind of prejudice, by little and little, wore off and they began to like it as well as the others and now, I believe, there was hardly a man in the Ship that did not attribute our being so free of the Scurvy to the Beer and Vegetables. . . .'

Soon after their arrival on Thursday, 1 April 1773, they began to brew beer beside the stream which entered the head of Ship Cove (plate 125). The setting was picturesque and the ingredients at hand. Cook wrote, 'we first made a strong decoction of the leaves or small branches of the Spruce tree★ (plate 126) & Tea shrub† (plate 127) by boiling them three or four hours, or untill the bark will strip with ease from the branches, then take the leaves or branches out of the Copper and mix with the liquor the proper quantity of Melasses and Inspissated Juce, one Gallon of the former and three of the latter is sufficient to make a Puncheon or 80 gallons of Beer, let this mixture just boil and then put it into the Cask and to it add an equal quantity of Cold Water more or less according to your taste and the strength of the decoction, when the whole is but milk warm put in a little grounds of Beer or yeast, if you have any, or any thing else that will cause fermentation and in a few days the Beer will be fit to drink. . . .' The beer was too astringent if rimu alone was used, but if manuka was added the 'Beer was exceeding Palatable and esteemed by every one on board'.

Anders Sparrman, who seems to have been the ship's gourmet, described it thus—'After a small amount of rum or arrack has been added, with some brown sugar, and stirred into this really pleasant, refreshing, and healthy drink, it bubbled and tasted rather like champagne.' Though its antiscorbutic properties could not have been very great it served its purpose and Cook was delighted that it helped to maintain the health of his people while providing them with some pleasure.

On the morning of Monday, 29 March 1773, some of the officers rowed a mile or two to the entrance of Cascade Cove. They returned almost

★Rimu, *Dacrydium cupressinum*.
†Manuka, *Leptospermum scoparium*.

Plate 126 (right). *"The Spruce Fir of New Zeeland". An engraving made from George Forster's drawing of the rimu* (Dacrydium cupressinum).

Plate 127 (far right). *An engraving from Forster's drawing of the tea plant, or manuka* (Leptospermum scoparium).

Plate 128. *"Family in Dusky Bay, New Zeland". An engraving from a drawing by William Hodges.*

immediately to report that they had seen a group of natives. A heavy shower of rain cleared about noon after which a small double canoe, containing eight people, appeared near Heron Island and somewhat hesitantly approached to within musket shot of the *Resolution*. It retreated again and later Cook took a boat and followed to Cascade Cove. He found two small round huts, several nets and some fish ready for cooking in the fireplaces. Though the Maoris had disappeared he left them some medals (which had been struck especially for this expedition), some beads and mirrors and, later, a hatchet, but did not 'force an interview' leaving the timing of such a meeting to the natives.

This eventually took place on the evening of Tuesday, 6 April 1773, when Cook, the Forsters and William Hodges were being rowed back from a visit to Duck Cove on the south coast of Resolution Island. The pinnace was threading its way through the islets between Indian and Long Islands when a faint halloo echoed across the waters. Cook ordered his boat to be rowed quietly towards the north-west point of Indian Island for he could see a small group of Maoris there (plate 128). As they approached they saw a well-built man of medium height (plate 129) dressed in a flaxen cloak standing on a little rocky promontory. He was leaning on his taiaha, a club 5 or 6 feet in length which often denoted the rank of chief, and, understandably, showed signs of apprehension. Behind him at the edge of the bush were two women each clutching an 18-foot bird spear. George Forster described the historic meeting— 'Captain Cook went to the head of the boat, called to him in a friendly manner, and threw him his own and some other handkerchiefs, which he would not pick up. The captain then taking some sheets of white paper in his hand, landed on the rock unarmed, and held the paper out to the native. The man now trembled very visibly, and having exhibited strong marks of fear in his countenance, took the paper: upon which captain Cook coming up to him, took hold of his hand, and

Plate 129 (top). "Old man, New Zeland". A portrait, in red crayon, made by William Hodges, probably represents the Maori chief in Dusky Bay.

Plate 130 (right). "Woman, New Zeland". This portrait, by William Hodges, is believed to portray the voluble young woman in Dusky Bay.

102

Plate 131. *The cave-dwelling in Cascade Cove. The site of an old Maori encampment, where human bones were found, which corresponded in development with the ages of the members of the family described by Cook.*

embraced him, touching the man's nose with his own, which is their mode of salutation.'

There followed a lively half hour of 'chit-chat which was little understood on either side in which the youngest of the two women bore by far the greatest share, which occasion'd one of the Seamen to say, that weomen did not want tongue in no part of the world. . . .' With kindness and generosity Captain Cook made friends with this Maori family so that they moved their camp from Indian Island to Pickersgill Harbour where they settled down across the cove from the *Resolution*. The man had two wives and, according to Clerke, 'one jolly Wench of a Daughter' (plate 130), a boy of about 14 years and three little children of whom the youngest was at the breast.

The Maoris of the south differed significantly from those Cook had met in the north. He, and his scientists, gave a detailed account of their appearance, their weapons and their tools, their speech, their habitations and canoes and their way of life. This was the more important, and poignant, as no one ever made contact with the Maoris of this district again. The picture given to us of this small group is both 'hail' and 'farewell'.

The first Polynesian people to reach New Zealand brought with them no edible roots or vegetables. They depended for food on the birds of the bush and the fish of the sea. In the south, giant moas still survived and, as piles of their bones at the mouths of the Waiau and Waitaki Rivers testify, they were killed and eaten in their

thousands. After the moas had been destroyed the Maoris ate fish, seals, shellfish, eels and birds, and occasionally rats and dogs, together with ferns and edible plants. They moved from the sea, through river valleys, to the mountains following seasonal food supplies till driven back to the coast by the winter weather. Never settling in a permanent home, they moved constantly from camp to camp. Their's was an arduous life and there was little time for fighting.

After the coming of the 'Great Fleet' to the warmer North Island, settlements of Maoris sprang up around their cultivated fields of kumara, taro and yam. The soil had to be prepared and the crops tended before they yielded their harvest. With this came the need to guard and defend their land from their neighbours. Thus an ordered society developed with villages and fortifications, with rank and status for the individual, alliances and power groups for the tribe and a deep devotion, which still persists, to the land. The northern tribes, practised in the arts of war, drove their weaker neighbours southwards to fight and harry the original inhabitants of the south.

Captain Cook noted the essential differences between the northern and southern Maoris— though he rightly pointed out that they were merely sections of the same people. 'The Inhabitants of this Bay are of the same race as those in the other parts of this Country, speak the same language and observe nearly the same customs . . .' He went on—'the many vestigias we saw of People

Plate 132. "Waterfall in Dusky Bay, New Zealand". This oil painting of the waterfall in Cascade Cove was made by William Hodges, from one of his sketches, in 1775.

in different parts of this Bay indicates that they live a wandering life never remaining long in one spott, and if one can judge from appearences & circumstances few as they are they live not in perfect amity one family with another. . . .' He wondered what 'could induce three or four families to seperate themselves so far from the Society of the rest of their fellow creatures. . . .'

With considerable insight George Forster suggested an answer to this question, 'This war-like disposition, together with the irascible temper of the whole nation, that cannot brook the least injury, is probably the cause which has induced this single family, and the few in the long inlet we had visited, to separate from the rest of their fellow creatures.'

Maori tradition has it that the family which Cook met in Dusky Sound was one of the remnants of the Ngati-Mamoe which wandered through the forests and along the coasts of Fiordland. The chief, who was befriended by Cook, was named Maru, originally a chief of the Ngati-Kuri who had defeated the Ngati-Mamoe in their pa at Preservation Inlet, and who followed them to their last retreat in Dusky Sound. It was the custom of the warriors to kill the males and capture the females—which might explain the form of the family known to Cook.

On 20 April 1773, the Maori family left their camp in Pickersgill Harbour and headed their canoe for Cascade Cove. They were never seen again. Significantly it was reported that Maru had waved his hatchet as if 'going to kill men'. The *Resolution* remained in the western part of Dusky Bay for another 2 weeks and, had they been able, there is no doubt that the Maoris would have returned to accept further gifts from the generous sailors. Cook was surprised and a little hurt that they did not reappear but Anders Sparrman wondered if they had been killed by marauders because of the axes and spike nails which represented untold wealth to envious eyes. Perhaps he was right. A few years ago human bones were found in a cave in Cascade Cove where there was evidence of a cannibal feast (plate 131). The bones of the victims corresponded in age with the male members of the Maori family. And hidden away in a cranny at the back of the cave was found 1 pound of oxidised wrought iron which may have been what remained of the axes or spikes given to the family by the Europeans. This can be no more than surmise as that lonely family was the last of the line in Dusky Sound. With their deaths their secrets were locked away for ever in the cliffs and chasms of their homeland (plate 132).

William Wales had been charged with the tasks of navigational research. This was no sinecure and entailed a great deal of hard, slogging work. After the *Resolution* had been moored, Wales went ashore and chose the promontory immediately north of the ship as the place for his observatory. It rose about 50 feet above sea level and was named Astronomers Point (plate 133). He and two men from the ship cut and cleared about an acre of virgin bush. He wrote 'many of the Trees which we were obliged to fell would have made fore-

Masts for the ship.' They cleared all the trees and shrubs which would have obscured the northern sky and, less completely, 'a vista towards the South for observing Stars South of the zenith'.

The observatory was set up at the highest point and erected over the ground on which had been placed a footing of stones. Wales was chagrined that even this did not provide a solid base for his instruments so he set them on two tree stumps cut for the purpose. This proved satisfactory and, after many observations of the sun, moon and stars, he calculated the position of Astronomers Point to lie in longitude 166° 18′ 9″ east, latitude 45° 47′ 26″ south. A modern estimation is, longitude 166° 33′ 56″ east of Greenwich and latitude 45° 47′ 45″ south of the equator. Cook was as yet unconvinced of the accuracy of Kendall's watch though he admitted that it was 'more owing to its rate of going not being well settled than to any bad quallities in the Watch'.

Meanwhile the naturalists had been busy in an environment completely new to European eyes. They collected botanical specimens wherever they went and studied the birds and fish. They even investigated a report from one of the seamen that he had seen a quadruped, something like an otter or fox. Captain Cook wrote it was 'about the size of a large Catt' and it seems likely that it was the

Plate 133. *Ship Cove today, with Astronomers Point to the left. Stretching away through the distant mountains is the passage now known as Cook Channel.*

Plate 134 (left). *The bush hawk, or New Zealand falcon* (Falco novaeseelandiae) *painted by George Forster.*

Plate 135 (above). *The grey duck* (Anas superciliosa superciliosa), *by George Forster.*

Plate 136 (left). Gentiana saxosa. *A painting by George Forster.*

Plate 137 (above). "Epacris pumila" (Pentachondra pumila). *A botanical painting, by George Forster.*

Plate 138. *A kokopu, or native trout. This specimen was captured and described by Johann Forster. George Forster made a painting of it with such accuracy that R. M. McDowall has been able to identify the species as* Galaxias argenteus.

Plate 139. *The moki, or bastard trumpeter* (Latridopsis ciliaris), *by George Forster.*

ship's cat on one of its foraging expeditions.

Johann Forster would write a description of each specimen and his son would record it with a detailed sketch (plates 134–141). Anders Sparrman spent his time botanising, though he also described some of the foods he tasted. After the formal account of the bush hawk he declared it was 'really delicious roasted' (plate 134). One of the first new plants he found was growing above the bushline when he climbed a formidable peak behind Cascade Cove. 'Half way up', wrote Sparrman, 'I discovered for the first time a *gynandrist* which I named *Forstera* after my fellow botanist, and have described it in *Acta Upsaliensa.*' George

Forster made a delicate drawing of the specimen which is now to be found in the Botanical Institute in Leningrad (plate 140). He also sketched the branch of a cabbage tree which Sparrman had collected on the mountain (plate 141).

Though it has frequently been said that the Forsters pirated the work of Banks and Solander there is no doubt that they carried out a tremendous amount of first-class, original work in Dusky Bay. They methodically described and dated their work and sketches, and, with a touch of genius, George Forster wrote in phonetic script the Maori name of the birds he drew. As these names and pronunciations could only have been given him by the

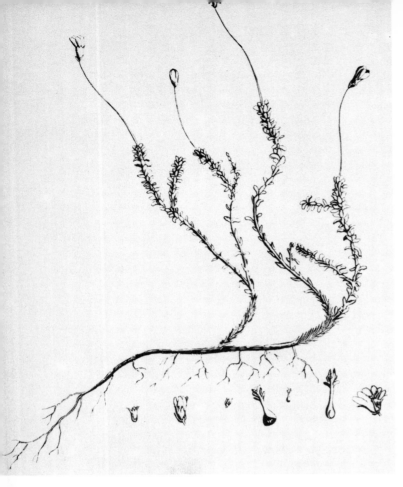

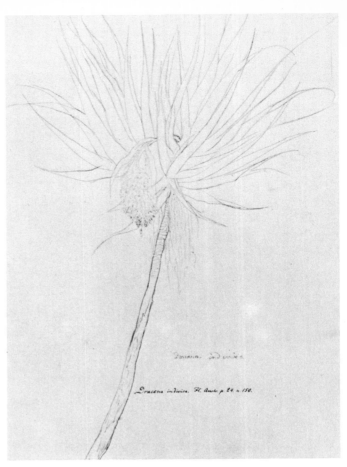

Plate 140. Forstera sedifolia. *This plant was collected by Anders Sparrman, and drawn by George Forster. The Latin inscription, written in the hand of George Forster may be translated as "It lives on the topmost peaks of the highest mountains of the South Island of New Zealand".*

Plate 141. *The broad-leaved cabbage tree (Cordyline indivisa). George Forster probably made this sketch from a specimen of the "dragon tree", brought back by Sparrman from his climb through the bush above Cascade Cove.*

Maori family, we can, through these phonetics, faintly hear the sound of the forgotten tongue of the southern Maori.

In a recent visit to Dusky Sound 13 different ferns were found on Astronomers Point. No fewer than seven of them had been collected, described and drawn by the Forsters. A fine flowering shrub, *Olearia oporina*, found only in Fiordland was the subject of a beautiful sketch, and a mountain daisy, *Celmisia holosericera*, still blooms today just above high-water mark where the Forsters first collected it. In the stream which runs into Ship Cove, Johann caught a native trout, *Galaxias argenteus*. He described it accurately and George painted it

(plate 138). These fish may still be found lurking in the same shady pools.

During the voyage the Forsters described 785 botanical specimens, 119 from New Zealand. While the *Resolution* lay in Dusky and Queen Charlotte Sounds they described and sketched 38 new species of birds and many fishes. Just as Solander and Banks laid the foundation of New Zealand botany, so the Forsters' work is the basis of our ornithology. After the *Resolution*'s return to England the Forsters had a bitter disagreement with the Admiralty over the premature publication of their account of the voyage, and they could never find employment again in England.

Many of their scientific and artistic works found their way to various European capitals. Despite their difficult natures, the Forsters contributed much to the success of the voyage and are deserving of more credit and respect than has been accorded them by posterity.

Captain Cook went methodically around Dusky Bay in the preparation of a superb and detailed survey. The map he drew in 1773 is still the best available for anyone sailing in these waters (plate 142). With his small boats and his hard worked oarsmen he explored all the coves, islands and inlets of the sound. He had some beautiful weather and it must have been a time of pleasure and relaxation. However, he felt it necessary to justify his charting activities, 'For although this country be far remote from the present trading part of the world, we can, by no means, tell what use future ages may make of the discoveries made in the present.' He need not have had fears about the usefulness of his chart for it caused southern New Zealand to be the focus of European effort for the next 50 years. The sealers, and later the whalers must have been grateful for his accurate survey of this lovely harbour.

Many celebrated navigators paid tribute to his work. Dr Archibald Menzies, who accompanied George Vancouver, wrote these words after he had journeyed round Dusky Bay, 'we could not help reflecting with peculiar pleasure & admiration

Plate 142. *"Dusky Bay in New Zeland 1773". By James Cook.*

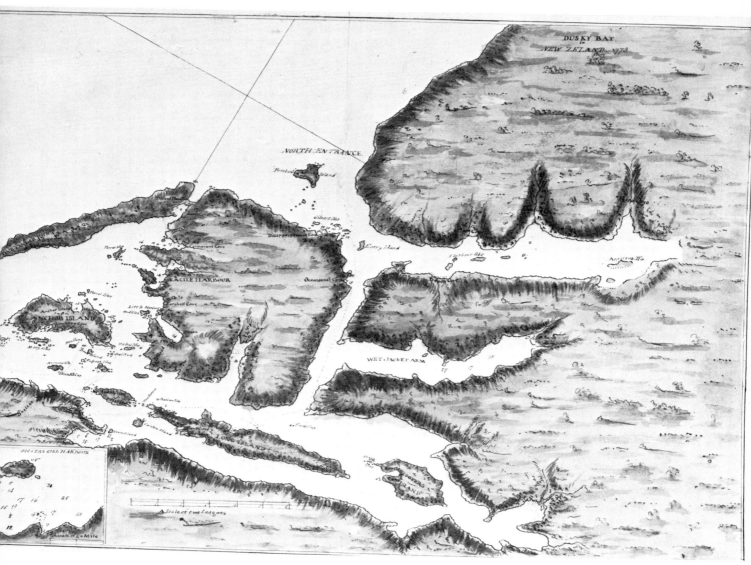

on the justness of his observations & the accuracy of his delineations throughout every part of the complicated survey of the extensive Sound.' And Robert Murry, who knew Dusky Sound in the eighteenth century better than any man, wrote, 'Where ever I have followed our immortal countryman, Capt. Cook, I have never been so presuming as to aim at description, he has left very little to be done at any Port, or on any Coast he ever visited.'

In New Zealand Cook is remembered for the speed, as well as the accuracy, of his running survey of the coast. On his first voyage 2,400 miles of coastline were charted in 6 months. So detailed and precise were his charts of the harbours he visited that many remained in use until recent times. One, the current Admiralty Chart No. 2589, which still bears the legend 'from Captain Cook's voyage of 1773', is of Pickersgill Harbour, Dusky Sound.

Cook's surveying expeditions (or 'marooning parties' as his seamen called them) allowed him to enjoy some excellent shooting in Dusky Bay. Many of the features of the sound were called after the birds which fell to his gun. Woodhen

Cove, Shag Islands, Duck Cove, Seal Isles, Cormorant Cove and Sportsman's Cove—a quiet landlocked harbour on Cooper Island—remind us of the success of his fowling expeditions. The game was cooked and eaten by the crew as a welcome addition to their diet. Oyster-catchers provided many welcome meals, and Cook noted that wekas which 'inhabet the Skirts of the Woods and feed upon the Sea beach, . . . are very like a Common Hen and eat very well in a Pye or Fricasee.'

He never forgot the threat of scurvy and he liberated some of the *Resolution's* geese at Goose Cove so that future mariners might have a source of fresh food. Unfortunately they did not thrive—perhaps because of the egg-robbing propensities of the hungry wekas. In addition, Cook tried to start a vegetable garden on Astronomers Point. 'In the evening I set fire to the top wood &ca that was on a part of the ground we had occupied in order to dry it, and in the morning dug it up and sowed in it several sorts of seeds, the ground was such as did not promise success to the planter and yet it was the best I could find.' This also proved a failure for the torrential rain and winds of Fiord-

land were too much for the vegetables.

And so, on Friday, 29 April 1773, the anchor was weighed and the *Resolution* left her comfortable mooring in Pickersgill Harbour and sailed eastwards towards the 'new Passage' (subsequently named Acheron Passage by Captain J. Lort Stokes who surveyed the sound in 1851 in a vessel of that name), to leave Dusky Bay by the northerly route. They were sad to leave that restful haven though Wales, who had suffered a series of colds, wrote 'we are now (thank God) leaving this dirty, and, on that Account, disagreeable Place.' Charles Clerke, however, wrote—'I cannot in gratitude take my final leave of this good Bay without doing some justice to its many good qualities . . . and I do think that Dusky Bay, for a Set of Hungry fellows after a long passage at Sea is as good as any place I've ever yet met with.'

George Forster summed up his thoughts in his fanciful way—'In a word, all around us we perceived the rise of arts, and the dawn of science, in a country which had hitherto lain plunged in one long night of ignorance and barbarism! But this pleasing picture of improvement was not to

last, and like a meteor, vanished as suddenly as it was formed. We re-imbarked all our instruments and utensils, and left no other vestiges of our residence, than a piece of ground, from whence we had cleared the wood.'

This piece of ground has remained relatively unaltered for 200 years. The fascination of Dusky Sound is that civilisation has passed it by. Pickersgill Harbour and Astronomers Point have not changed since the *Resolution* lay moored to the overhanging trees. The stumps left by Wales and his men are still visible on the site of his clearing (plate 143) and it is not difficult to trace its perimeter, for the original trees are much larger than those of the secondary growth. Progress and development have transformed nearly all the places of historic interest in New Zealand. But Dusky Sound is different. Its moment of greatness came with its discovery and its period of greatest activity occurred before the end of the eighteenth century. Since then it has been visited by the sealing gangs and the whalers, by a few prospectors and some fishermen, by two shipwrecked parties and a handful of tourists. Nothing has really changed in 200 years and the majesty of the mountains, the spectacular waterfalls,

Plate 145. *The north entrance to Dusky Bay. As the* Resolution *departed, William Hodges looked back and painted this picture of Breaksea Island, and the opening of Breaksea Sound.*

the hanging valleys and the perpendicular bush-clad walls of the sound, so vividly described by Cook and his men, may be equally enjoyed by the visitor today (plate 144).

Winds were light and variable as the *Resolution* worked her way to the Acheron Passage. It was not until Wednesday, 11 May 1773, that the ship cleared the northern entrance, or Breaksea Sound (plate 145). As is usual on this coast Cook met a huge south-west swell when he finally reached the open sea—'a prodigious swell from SW which broke with great voilence on all Shores which were exposed to it.'

Cook set a course for Queen Charlotte Sound and followed the coastline northwards with the high alps to the east rising above the bushline to their perpetual snow. By 16 May 1773, the *Resolution*, driven by a south-west gale had reached Cape Farewell and turned towards the strait. At 4 o'clock in the afternoon on Tuesday, 17 May 1773, when the ship was about 3 leagues from Stephens Island, an unusual danger threatened them; 'the sky became suddenly obscured and seemed to indicate much Wind which occasioned us to clew up all our sails, presently after Six Water Spouts were seen, four rose and spent themselves between us and the land, the fifth was at some distance without us and the Sixth pass'd under our Stern at about fifty yards from us, the diameter of the base of this spout I judged to be about fifty or sixty feet, during the time these Spouts lasted which was near a hour we had light puffs of wind from all points of the Compass.' There must have been great power in the whirl-winds to lift such a weight of water to the clouds and Wales was relieved at their escape. 'I am perswaded that if it had gone over her it would have torn away her sails & yards; perhaps her Masts and standing Rigging also.' Thankful for this escape Captain Cook continued eastwards towards Queen Charlotte Sound and his rendezvous with Captain Furneaux.

9 Queen Charlotte Sound

*We found the country not quite so steep as at the
southern extremity of New Zeeland . . . In most parts,
however, they [the hills] were covered with forests
equally intricate and impenetrable as those of Dusky
Bay*

George Forster

At daylight on the morning of Wednesday, 18 May 1773, the *Resolution* rounded Point Jackson and entered Queen Charlotte Sound eagerly searching for signs of the *Adventure*. She was at once greeted by the flash of guns from Furneaux's observatory on the 'Hippa Island', adjoining Motuara (plate 146), and both crews were overjoyed to see each other. Furneaux well knew Captain Cook's passion for fresh food and welcomed him appropriately. Lieutenant Burney recorded, 'at ½ past 10 Mr Kemp went out to her with fish and Sallad from the Garden in the Small Cutter. Every thing we Set in the garden is in a fair way—nothing has faild.'

The *Adventure* fired an 11-gun salute, which was returned by the *Resolution*. Next morning Cook anchored safely in Ship Cove (plate 147).

Captain Furneaux made a full report on his activities since the ships had been separated in the Southern Ocean, on 8 February 1773. As his search for the *Resolution* had proved fruitless he turned the *Adventure* towards New Zealand. He guessed that Cook would continue his search for the southern continent in high latitudes and he recalled Tasman's route to his north. Furneaux steered his ship about midway between in order to explore an unknown part of the ocean. On

Plate 146. *Motuara and the adjoining "Hippa Island", on which William Bayly set up his observatory. Beyond is Ship Cove sheltering beneath Mt. Furneaux and, to the right, Cannibal Cove.*

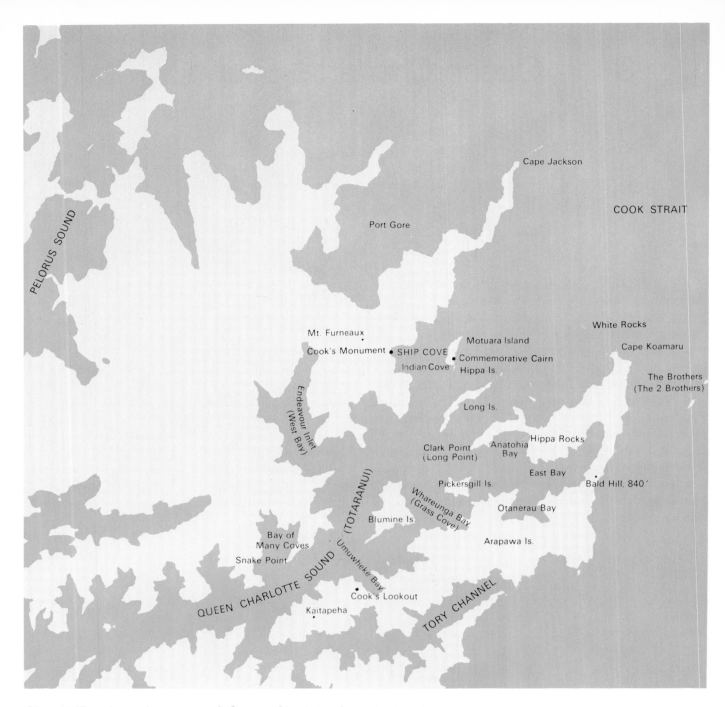

Plate 147. *A modern map of Queen Charlotte Sound, showing the area which was visited and mapped by Cook.*

Tuesday, 9 March 1773, he sighted Tasmania and 2 days later anchored in Adventure Bay. He continued up the eastern coast of Tasmania until 19 March 1773, and then turned east and 'haul'd up for New Zealand'. Furneaux remained unconvinced that Bass Strait existed but Bayly, the astronomer wrote—'& it seems very evident this is the mouth of a straight which Seperates new Holland from Van Diemans Land. . . .'

It was not until Sunday, 3 April 1773, that the *Adventure* entered Cook Strait and, after beating about against winds and tides for 4 days, entered Queen Charlotte Sound and anchored at Ship Cove on Wednesday, 6 April 1773. Captain Furneaux focused his activities on Motuara, erecting a hospital for some sick men, cultivating a vegetable garden and setting up the observatory on the adjoining 'Hippa Island'. Mr Bayly made

Plate 148. *The "Hippa Island" as seen today from Motuara. A navigation light on the summit now marks the site of Bayly's observatory.*

himself quite snug on this old Maori pa and described it thus, 'I went on Shore on a small Island called the Hippa by the Natives which I named Observatory Island, it is a rock whose sides are perpendicular in many places, & indeed the whole was well fortified by nature there being only one landing place, & the passage up from it exceeding difficult, but by hard labour I made steps in the rocks so that its ascent was much easier than before—on the top of this small Island was a Town consisting of 33 houses, the most elevated part was tolerably level for about 100 Yards long & 8 or 10 Yards wide; this was fortified with strong posts or sticks drove into the ground, & those interwoven with long sticks in a horizontal direction, & then filled with small brush wood with one place two feet square where was a wooden dore, so that only one man could get in at a time & that on his hands & knees & of course easy destroy'd if at war.'

The hippa or pa was deserted but the old Maori houses, the floor dug a foot or more below ground level for warmth at night, proved very comfortable and provided accommodation for the men of the observatory. Cook described this little island as 'joined to Motuara at low water' but today the channel is about 4 feet wide at all phases of the tide. It is even possible to manoeuvre a dinghy between Motuara and the 'Hippa Island'.

This islet rises about 80 feet above the sea at its highest point and may now be ascended by con-

crete steps built to provide access to a small unmanned lighthouse which stands where the old village stood. It is very likely that the steps are in the place where Bayly cut his original pathway for the sides of the island are still as perpendicular as they were in Bayly's time (plate 148). The 33 houses must have been crowded together on the summit ridge and, according to Webber's sketch in 1777, on the slopes above the cliffs, for the area of the pa seems rather less than Bayly's estimation. This effect may in part be due to the extensive regrowth of vegetation since the Maoris' occupation. Though once cleared inside the palisade, as shown in Webber's painting, the island is now covered by shrubs and trees up to 20 feet or so in height. The manuka, five-finger, wineberry, fern, coprosma and hebe completely hide the place where Bayly tended his garden (plate 149). The observatory site, however, overlooks the entrance of the sound and it is easily seen why the arrival of the *Resolution* was first observed by the astronomers on the 'Hippa Island'.

Before Cook arrived, the *Adventure* had been stripped in preparation for a comfortable stay throughout the winter. But Cook had other ideas and he directed Captain Furneaux to refit his ship for a winter cruise through the central Pacific.

Cook was interested and a little disappointed that he could not find his old Maori friends of the first voyage. 'I was lead into these reflections, by not being able to recollect the face of any

Plate 149. *The top of the "Hippa Island", once the site of a fortified Maori village, is now covered by a dense growth of native bush. Beyond, the slope of Motuara and the hills of Point Jackson may be compared with the painting of this place made by Webber in 1777 (Plate 172).*

Plate 150. *The sweet potato or kumara (Ipomoea batatas), a painting made by Sydney Parkinson, in Tahiti, in 1769. This plant was brought to New Zealand by the Polynesians, and formed an important part of the Maori diet.*

one person I had seen here three years ago, nor hath it appear'd that any one of them had the least knowledge of me or any other person with me that was here at that time, it is therefore not very improbable but that the greatest part of the Inhabitants that were here in the beginning of the year 1770 are drove out of it or have on their own accord removed some were else; certain it is that not one third the people are here now that were then. Their Strong hold on the point of Moutara hath been some time deserted and we find many forsaken habetation in all parts of the Sound, however we are not wholly to infer from this that this place has been once very populous for each family may, for their own conveniency when

they move from place to place, have more hutts than one or two.'

There were some very discerning observations made about the differences in the way of life of the South Island Maoris from that of the North Islanders. Furneaux, while visiting Tolaga Bay some time afterwards, wrote 'The natives here are the same as those of Charlottes Sound, but more numerous and seemed settled, having regular Plantations of Sweet Potatoes and other roots which are very good.' The stable village life, around the cultivated land, contrasted with the nomadic habits of the South Islanders. Captain Cook wrote '. . . for it is very common for them when they even go but a little way to carry their whole property with them, every place being equally alike to them if it affords the necessary subsistance so that it can hardly be said that they are ever from home, thus we may easily account for the migration of those few small families we found in Dusky Bay. Living thus dispers'd in small parties knowing no head but the chief of the family or tribe whose authority may be very little, subjects them to many inconveniences a well regulated society united under one head, or any other form of government, are not subject to.' The ordered communities of the north 'form Laws and regulations for their general security, are not alarm'd at the appearence of every stranger and if attack'd or invaded by a publick enimy have strong holds to retire to where they can with advantage defend themselves, their property & their Country.' The wandering South Island Maoris, however, 'by living a wandering life in small parties are distitute of most of these advantages which subjects them to perpetual alarms, and we generally find them upon their guard travelling and working as it were with their Arms in their hands.'

The key to the position was the fact that the kumara and taro did not thrive in the colder climates of the South Island and could not be cultivated south of Banks Peninsula (plate 150). Cook saw the importance of providing the Maoris with a root vegetable which could be successfully grown in the cooler regions. George Forster described Cook's efforts to introduce potatoes. 'Captain Cook, who was determined to omit nothing which might tend to the preservation of European garden-plants in this country, prepared the soil, sowed seeds, and transplanted the young plants in four or five different parts of this sound. He had cultivated a spot of ground on the beach of Long Island, another in the Hippah rock, two more on Motu-aro, and one of considerable extent at the bottom of Ship Cove, where our vessels lay at anchor. He chiefly endeavoured to raise such vegetables as have useful and nutritive roots, and among them particularly potatoes, of which we had been able to preserve but few in a state of vegetation. He had likewise sown corn of several sorts, beans, kidney-beans, and pease, and devoted the latter part of his stay in great measure to these occupations.'

Not only did he have to prepare and plant the gardens but he had to arouse some interest in the Maoris to tend the crops. On Saturday, 29 May 1773, he took a Maori chief over to Motuara and 'shew'd him the Potatoes planted there by Mr Fannen the Master of the *Adventure* which he had brought from the Cape of Good Hope, there seems to be no doubt of their succeeding as they were in a very thriving state, the man was so pleased with them that he immidiately began to hough the earth about the plants, I call'd them Coumalla a root common in many parts of Eahei nomauwe and is as I could find from this man not unknown to the Inhabitents of Tavai-poenammoo. I next carried him to the other of Captain Furneaux's gardens (this gentleman being with me) I explaned to him as well as I could the nature of the Turnips, Carrots & Parsnips roots together with Potatoes that will be of more use to them than all the other vegetables. I gave him a tolerable Idea of the Carrots and Parsnips by calling them Tara a root to which they bear some likeness and is known to the Natives.'

In addition to the gift of vegetables to the Maoris, Captain Cook had also brought out on the *Resolution* a number of domesticated animals which he proposed to liberate for the benefit of the natives. The first attempt to introduce sheep to New Zealand ended in failure. A ram and a ewe, the only ones remaining from the sheep taken aboard at the Cape of Good Hope, were put ashore at Ship Cove. On 23 May 1773, Cook wrote, 'Last Night the Ewe and Ram I had with so much care and trouble brought to this place, died, we did suppose that they were poisoned by eating of some poisonous plant, thus all my fine hopes of stocking this Country with a breed of Sheep were blasted in a moment.'

At Ship Cove there is a pleasant grove of karaka trees (*Corynocarpus laevigatus*) which were no doubt planted by the Maoris as the berries provided them with seasonal food. The raw berries are poisonous to both man and dogs and the Maoris were careful to bake the berries slowly in their ovens to destroy the toxic substance. Sheep and cattle, however, are not affected and it seems likely that tutu (*Coriaria arborea*), which has killed so many New Zealand sheep and which still grows in Ship Cove, was the cause of the death of the sheep which Cook had nursed through scurvy in Dusky Bay and had brought with such care and difficulty through the rigours of the Antarctic Seas (plate 151).

About 10 days later Cook, Furneaux and Johann Forster were rowed over to East Bay where they put ashore a male and female goat. Captain

Plate 151. *Tutu* (Coriaria arborea) *still flourishes along the banks of the stream at Ship Cove, and karaka trees* (Corynocarpus laevigatus) *grow on the flat land round the monument. Groves of tree ferns, on the hillside behind, indicate where the bush was felled by the explorers for timber to repair their ships.*

this liberty of the Boy offended old Will the Ram Goat who up with his head and knock'd the boy backwards on the Deck, Will would have repeated his blow had not some of the people got to the boys assistance, this missfortune however seem'd to him irreparable, the Shirt was dirted and he was afraid to appear in the Cabbin before his father untill brought in by Mr Forster, when he told a very lamentable story against Goure the great Dog, for so they call all the quadrepeds we have aboard, nor could he be pacified till his shirt was wash'd and dry'd.'

Potatoes and pigs were the Europeans' greatest gifts to the southern Maoris and would provide them not only with a nutritious food but also with a more stable life and, later, with produce which they could sell to visiting sailors.

But civilisation also brought disadvantages. Ferocious and destructive black rats had been inadvertently carried out from Europe by the *Endeavour* and had become 'enormously abundant', dispossessing the gentler, herbivorous native rats from their territory. Captain Cook also recorded that the morals of the Maoris had sadly deteriorated as a result of contact with the Europeans. 'Such are the concequences of a commerce with Europeans and what is still more to our Shame civilized Christians, we debauch their Morals already too prone to vice and we interduce among them wants and perhaps diseases which they never before knew and which serves only to disturb that happy tranquillity they and their fore Fathers had injoy'd.' He knew his men were introducing venereal disease but was unaware of the effect tuberculosis would have on these susceptible people. The traffic in firearms was to come later.

Another cause of some disappointment to Cook was a slight discrepancy between the results of the determination of longitude on the two voyages. Very honestly, but with some reluctance, Captain Cook admitted that his estimation of the longitude of Queen Charlotte Sound, made during the first voyage, was a little astray. As a result of many observations William Bayly had calculated that the longitude of the 'Hippa Island', on the second voyage, was $173° 48' 55\frac{1}{2}''$ east, and Cook conceded that 'they corrispond with Mr Wales's observations made in Dusky Bay reduced to this place by the Watches.' Wales's estimation of Queen Charlotte Sound was $174° 25' 07\frac{1}{2}''$ east, which, though nearer Cook's figure, still showed that the sound was originally placed too far to the east.

Furneaux had previously liberated a boar and sow in Cannibal's Cove. Hopefully, Captain Cook wrote, 'there is no great danger that the Natives will destroy them as they are exceedingly afraid of both', and, 'The Goats will undoubtedly take to the Mountains and the Hoggs to the Woods where there is plenty of food for both.' The natives' fear of the animals would not have been lessened by an episode involving 'Will the Ram Goat'. A Maori brought his son on board and asked to be given a shirt—as Cook recorded the event—'which I accordingly did the Boy was so fond of his new dress that he went all over the Ship presenting him self to every boddy that came in his way,

10 The Winter Voyage

Circumstances seem to point out to us that there is none [Southern Continent] but this is too important a point to be left to conjector, facts must determine it and these can only be had by viseting the remaining unexplored parts of this Sea

James Cook

Cook put his plan for the winter voyage before Furneaux—'to proceed immidiately to the East between the Latitudes of 41° and 46° untill I arrived in the Longitude 140° or 135° West and then, providing no land was discovered, to proceed to Otaheite, from thence to return back to this place by the Shortest rout.' It was all part of the master plan and, though he did not expect to find a Southern Continent, he was determined to make certain—one way or the other.

The ships put to sea at 7 a.m. on the morning of Monday, 7 June 1773 and, after a tussle with the Cook Strait tides, were wafted by a north-west wind into the Pacific. They sailed down to the 47th parallel and then worked their way eastwards until they reached 133° 30′ west of Greenwich. It was the middle of the southern winter, the winds were heavy and the crew constantly wet. Cook had proved to his satisfaction that there was no large land mass in these seas and without regrets the ships turned north for Tahiti. Scurvy had unexpectedly appeared and Cook redoubled his efforts to prevent further disease as he hurried northwards. On 16 August 1773, the ships were off Tahiti and the men enjoyed coconuts and bananas and, perhaps, the 'greens' which the island pro-

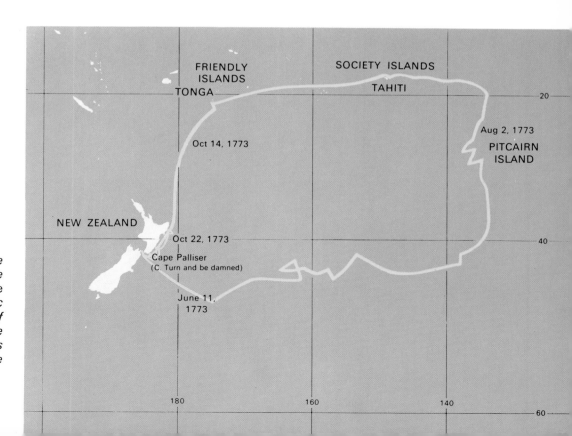

Plate 152. *Map of the Winter Voyage of the* Resolution *and* Adventure *through the central Pacific Ocean. Towards the end of this voyage the ships were separated by violent winds off the east coast of the North Island.*

Plate 153. *An aerial view looking west across the entrance to Wellington Harbour. The "black Rocks", or Barrett's Reef, may be seen near the centre of the channel and, in the distance, The Brothers, and the entrance to Queen Charlotte Sound (top left).*

vided. Some of the smaller islands of the Society Group were visited, where there was plenty of food and a very real affection for Captain Cook. Though there was some thieving Cook meted out justice and enhanced his reputation for fair-minded humanity. They sailed west to Tonga and met a friendly reception with trading and barter and an exchange of hospitality. Cook named these islands the Friendly Isles.

The ships were ordered to sea on 7 October 1773, and Cook headed south for New Zealand. He had acquired adequate provisions and, in addition, had invited two natives of the Society Islands to accompany him. Cook was host to Odiddy, an attractive young man, who learned the Maori language and was to prove a useful interpreter. Furneaux carried Omai, a youth who was subsequently lionised by London society.

Gales blew up when the ships were approaching the New Zealand coast and they lost touch with each other on 22 October 1773. Two days later the *Adventure* rejoined the *Resolution* off Cape Palliser. It was not for long as another storm struck. 'The aspect of the ocean was at once magnificent and terrific,' wrote George Forster, 'now on the summit of a broad and heavy billow, we overlooked an immeasurable expanse of sea, furrowed into numberless deep channels; now on a sudden the wave broke under us, and we plunged into a deep and dreary valley, whilst a fresh mountain rose to windward with a foaming crest, and threatned to overwhelm us'. Though the *Adventure* was blown out into the Pacific, Cook hung on close to the south coast of the North Island, and on Wednesday, 2 November 1773, he saw a deep inlet—'which had all appearance of a good Harbour. Being tired with beating against the obstinate NW winds I resolved (if I found it practical) to

Plate 154 (top). *The obverse of the medal struck for Cook's second voyage.*

Plate 155 (lower). *The reverse of the medal showing the* Resolution *and* Adventure.

put into this place or to anchor in the Bay which lies before it. . . .' He anchored about a mile from Barrett's Reef at the mouth of Wellington Harbour (plate 153). 'Soon after we had anchored several of the Natives came off to us in three Canoes, two from the one shore and one from the other, it required but little address to get three or four aboard to whom I distributed midals and nails, the latter they were extravigancly fond of, I also gave to one man two cocks and two hens, these he recieved with such indifferency as gave me little hopes that proper care would be taken of them.' It is almost certain that the *Resolution* would have entered Wellington Harbour if the *Adventure* had been in company. Instead, Cook headed for Queen Charlotte Sound in a north-east breeze which gradually developed into a southerly gale and did much damage to his sails. The anchor was dropped in Ship Cove, Queen Charlotte Sound on Thursday, 3 November 1773.

The medals he gave to the Maoris who visited the ship at Wellington Heads were similar to those he had distributed to chiefs in Dusky Bay and Queen Charlotte Sound. In his journal he wrote, 'These medals are to be given to the natives of new discovered countries and left there as testimonies of our being the first discoverers.' George Forster described the medals. 'Among these was a number of brass medals, gilt, about one inch and three-quarters in diameter, which had been struck on purpose to be left as a memorial of this voyage among the nations we should meet with: on one side was the head of his present majesty, with the inscription, GEORGE III KING OF GREAT BRITAIN, FRANCE, AND IRELAND &c (plate 154). On the reverse, the representation of two men of war, with the names RESOLUTION and ADVENTURE over them: and the exergue SAILED FROM ENGLAND MARCH MDCCLXXII' (plate 155). They were presumably minted before the sailing date had been delayed.

It is of great interest that some of the medals Cook distributed during his second voyage have been found in various parts of the South Island. One was found by Mr T. D. McManaway at Rams Head, Pelorus Sound, one was found by Mrs J. W. Hunter on Murdering Beach near Dunedin, one was found at Kartigi, one at Otanerau Bay in Queen Charlotte Sound, another was found at Tuna Bay, Pelorus Sound, and a sixth on the banks of the Wairau River near Blenheim. One other was kept by Anders Sparrman and is now in the Ethnographical Museum of Sweden in Stockholm. Attached to it is a note which Sparrman is thought to have written. Translated it reads 'Medal struck in commemoration of the voyage round the earth to the South Pole, for presentation to the kings of the Indians.'

Once the *Resolution* was safely anchored in Queen Charlotte Sound, Captain Cook directed the energies of his men towards fitting out the ship for the summer voyage into the Antarctic. He had been away from Ship Cove from the first week in June until 3 November 1773. Though it had been the winter season Cook found that his gardens had flourished—not through the diligence of the Maoris, who had neglected them, but more because of the beneficence of nature and because the gardens had been well-sited to guard against frost damage. Nevertheless, the Maoris seemed to have recognised the possibilities of potatoes. After inspecting all the gardens George Forster was able to report, 'We found all the radishes and turneps shot into seed, the cabbages and carrots very fine, and abundance of onions and parsley in good order; the peas and beans were almost entirely lost, and seemed to have been destroyed by rats. The potatoes were likewise all extirpated; but, from appearances, we guessed this to have been the work of the natives'.

Forster was also most impressed with the potential value of the native flax plant which grew so luxuriantly on the islands in the sound. 'No plant promises to become so useful to Europe by transplantation as this flag. The hemp or flax which the New Zeelanders make of it, is excessively strong, soft, glossy, and white; and that which has been prepared again in England, has almost equalled silk in lustre. It grows on all kinds of soil, and, being perennial, may be cut down to the root every year, and requires scarce any attendance or care in the cultivation'. On 4 November 1773 he painted a picture of this useful plant (plate 156).

The Maoris visited the ship and provided the crew with fresh fish. They built their little huts and settled down in a cove just to the south of Ship Cove, which George Forster called Indian Cove. They indulged themselves in some profitable pilfering which Cook accepted with remarkable good humour. Some canoes arrived with about 100 Maoris who stole six small water casks before beating a hurried retreat in the early hours of the morning. Though presumably unfamiliar with

pockets the Maoris soon developed a very skilful technique for picking them. A number of natives were around Captain Cook practising the art when he expostulated at this evil 'an evil which one of the chiefs undertook to remove, and with fury in his eyes made a shew of keeping the people at a proper distance, I applauded his conduct but at the same time kept so good a lookout as to detect him in picking my Pocket of a handkerchief, which I suffered him to put in his bosom before I seem'd to know any thing of the matter and then told him what I had lost, he seemed quite ignorant and inicent, till I took it from him, and then he put it off with a laugh, and he had acted his part with so much address that it was hardly possible for me to be angery with him, so that we remained good friends and he accompanied me on board to dinner. . . .'

There was some anxiety in the minds of the Maoris of Indian Cove which appeared to centre around a raid which their own men were making on some tribe in Admiralty Bay. The marauders had losses, as was shown by the self-inflicted cutting of the legs by which the women showed their grief, but claimed a great victory with 50 of the enemy dead. One youth of the Admiralty Bay tribe who had been killed in battle provided a grisly meal for the victors. The officers saw the Maoris eating some of the flesh, but Cook himself wanted to be 'an eyewittness to a fact which many people had their doubts about'. He ordered a piece of human flesh 'to be broiled and brought on the quarter deck where one of these Canibals eat it with a seeming good relish before the whole ships Company which had such effect on some of them as to cause them to vomit.' Odiddy was overcome with horror and though he had previously been good friends with some of the Maoris 'now he neither would come near them or suffer them to touch him'.

Cook himself could look objectively. He had proved beyond doubt that the Maoris were cannibals, but they also had good qualities—'. . . the New Zealanders are certainly in a state of civilization, their behaviour to us has been Manly and Mild, shewing always a readiness to oblige us; they have some arts among them which they execute with great judgement and unweared patience: they are far less addicted to thieving than the other Islanders and are I believe strictly honist among them-selves. This custom of eating their enimies slain in battle (for I firmly believe they eat the flesh of no others) has undoubtedly been handed down to them from the earliest times and we know that it is not an easy matter to break a nation of its ancient customs let them be ever so inhuman and savage, especially if that nation is void of all religious principles as I believe the new zealanders in general are'.

He demonstrated his even-handed justice to the Maoris in a very practical way. One day a party of the ship's men came on a little hut in the bush which contained the natives' horde of treasure bartered or taken from the sailors. After the seamen had returned to the ship some Maoris came on board and complained that the sailors had stolen their goods. They picked on Richard Lee, seaman, as the person responsible. Cook immediately ordered the severe penalty of 12 lashes—a punishment given in front of the Maori witnesses. Cook wrote, 'It has ever been a maxim with me to punish the least crimes any of my people have committed against these uncivilized Nations, their robing us with impunity is by no means a sufficient reason why we should treat them in the same

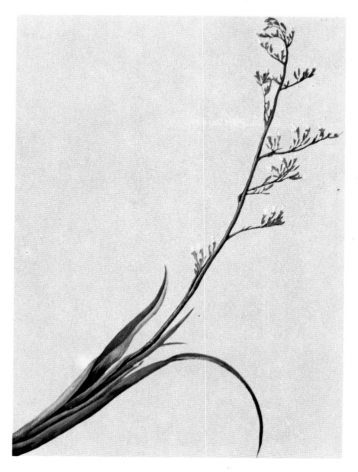

Plate 156 (left). *The New Zealand flax* (Phormium tenax). *Painting by George Forster.*

Plate 157 (above). Veronica elliptica, *by George Forster. This sketch of the veronica illustrates the accuracy and detail of Forster's botanical drawings.*

Plate 158. *The blue reef heron* (Demigretta matook). *This painting was made by George Forster, in Queen Charlotte Sound.*

manner. . . .'

It may have been Cook's upbringing on a farm that made him so anxious to provide the New Zealanders with farm animals. Certain it is that Cook was very skilful in his care of the livestock he carried on his ship. It is indeed remarkable how many of them survived their cramped quarters, their restricted diet and the storms and cold of the southern voyages. Cook had a practical knowledge of this which must have been most unusual in the Royal Navy. The work of acclimatisation had been planned as a result of his observations

from the *Endeavour*, but it was not until May 1773, when the *Resolution* first visited Queen Charlotte Sound, that pigs and goats had been liberated. Six months later, in November 1773, Cook was able to take stock of the position. He found one of Captain Furneaux's sows in Indian Cove, slightly lame but alive and well, but the boar and sow had been taken away and the two goats, it was stated, had been killed and eaten. Cook was disheartened, 'thus all our endeavours for stocking this Country with usefull Animals are likely to be frusterated by the very people whom we meant to serve. . . .'

Plate 159. *The tui* (Pros-themadera novaeseelandiae novaeseelandiae), *by George Forster. The tui was first described in Dusky Bay, but some birds were kept alive on a diet of sugar and water, and this painting was probably completed in Queen Charlotte Sound.*

On Monday, 21 November 1773, he tried again. He secretly took some animals into the bush and hid them so that they would be safe from the Maoris. 'I took four Hogs, three sows and one boar, two hens and three cocks and carried them a little way into the woods in the very bottom of West Bay where I left them with as much food as would serve them a week or ten days. This I did in order to keep them in the woods, least they should come down to the shore in search of food and be discovered by the natives'. He also deter-mined to 'leave some cocks and hens in the woods at Ship Cove, but these will have a chance of falling into the hands of the Natives whose wandering way of life will prevent them from breeding even Should they take proper care of them.'

Cook summed up the position. 'I have made mention of the Natives of Queen Charlottes Sound geting the three Hogs which Captain Furneaux put on shore; the young sow we know is in their possession but it is by no means certain that they got the old sow and boar, but even suppose they did by their own accounts they are yet alive and great reason to believe that they will take care of them and as to those I put on shore I have great reason to think they will never find. More Cocks and Hens are left behind than I know of as several of our people had of these as well as my self, some of which they put on shore and others they sold

to the Natives, whom we found took care enough of them. The two goats however I believe were killed.'

There was now real anxiety about the safety of the *Adventure*. On 15 November 1773, Cook took a party over to East Bay in the pinnace. George Forster wrote that they disembarked 'towards the bottom of the bay.' Leaving the naturalists botanising and collecting birds (plates 157–159), Cook climbed to the top of the same hill he had scaled in 1770—probably Bald Hill. Though visibility was not good Cook scanned the horizon carefully but without success, for any sign of the *Adventure*, 'as to the Adventure I dispair of seeing her any more but am totally at a loss to conceive what is become of her till now.' Cook recorded that the cairn that he had previously raised on the summit had been pulled down by the Maoris 'with a view of finding some thing hid in it'. They returned in thoughtful mood to the ship, paying a visit to the Maoris on the Hippa Rocks en route.

Cook left a message for Furneaux in case he should arrive after the departure of the *Resolution*. 'The morning before we sailed I wrote a memorandum seting forth the time we arrived last here, the day we sailed, the rout I intended to take & such other information as I thought necessary for Captain Furneaux to know and buried it in a

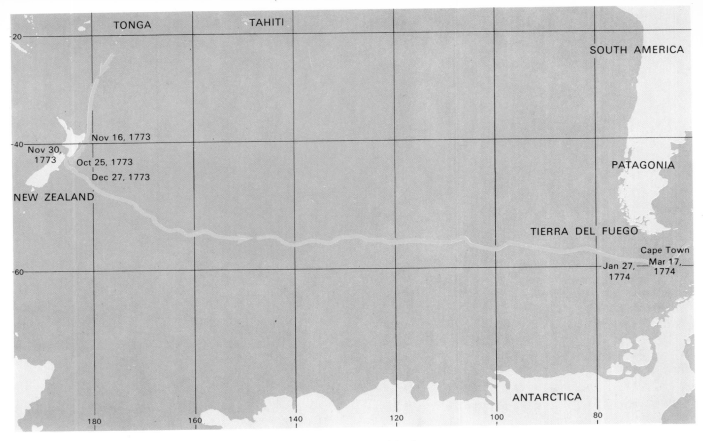

Plate 160. *Map of the* Adventure's *voyage. After contact with the* Resolution *had been lost, Captain Furneaux refitted in Queen Charlotte Sound, and then made a fast passage across the South Pacific Ocean to pass Cape Horn on his way home to England.*

bottle under the root of a tree in the garden in the bottom of the Cove. . . .' On the root was carved 'Look underneath'. Though Captain Cook was very disturbed about the loss of his consort he did not let this divert him from the master plan. 'Nevertheless this shall not discourage me from fully exploring the Southern parts of the Pacific Ocean in the doing of which I intend to employ the whole of the insuing season and if I do not find a Continent or isle between this and Cape Horn in which we can Winter perhaps I may spend the Winter within the Tropicks or else proceed round Cape Horn to Falkland Islands, such were my thoughts at this time, the execution of which will depend in a great Measure on circumstances which at this time it was not possible for me to fore see.'

The *Resolution* was now ready to sail and on Thursday, 25 November 1773, the anchor was weighed and the ship put out into the sound. By midday she was clear of the heads and moved over to the south of the North Island running along from point to point firing guns every half hour and searching the coast for signs of shipwreck or survivors. It was a rocky coast and he wrote, 'All the Land adjoining to the Sea between Cape Terawhitte and Cape Palliser is exceeding barren, probably occasioned by its being so much exposed to the Cold southerly winds.' After a thorough search Cook turned his ship towards the open sea. He wrote proudly of his men—'On our quiting the Coast and consequently all hopes of being joined by our consort, I had the satisfaction to find that not a man was dejected or thought the dangers we had yet to go through were in the least increased by being alone, but as cheerfully proceeded to the South or wherever I thought proper to lead them as if she or even more Ships had been in our Company.' By Saturday, 27 November 1773, the *Resolution* had sailed over 100 miles into the Pacific Ocean.

11 The Adventure

It might probably happen from Some quarrel, or the fairness of the Opportunity tempted them; our people being so very incautious & thinking themselves to Secure

James Burney

The *Adventure* limped into Ship Cove, Queen Charlotte Sound, on Tuesday, 30 November 1773, only 3 days after Cook had given up his search and had left the New Zealand coast. Captain Furneaux and his men had been buffeted around by adverse winds since he had been separated from the *Resolution* off Cape Palliser on 25 October 1773. He had been driven back to the north and had found some days of respite in Tolaga Bay where he rode out an uncomfortable gale. The ship sailed again on 16 November 1773, in an effort to reach Queen Charlotte Sound but, once more, 'met with several gales of wind off the mouth of the streights and continued beating backwards and forwards till the 30th of November when we were so fortunate as to get a favourable wind'. Lieutenant Burney wrote—'from our being so often baffled in trying to get round Cape Palliser our Seamen Christend it, by the significant name of Cape Turn and be damned . . .'

Once in Ship Cove they very soon found Cook's 'Look underneath' notice, dug up the bottle and read of the plans and departure of the *Resolution*.

Captain Furneaux could not immediately follow, however, as the bread had been damaged and had to be rebaked before it was fit for consumption. The ship, too, strained by the succession of gales required refitting before the long voyage home by Cape Horn. The Maoris supplied ample quantities of fresh fish and, as usual, stole any articles which appealed to them. One night, when a sentinel was dozing, they took everything out of the tents on shore and loaded them into a canoe. At the last moment the alarm was raised and the Maoris escaped, leaving their canoe. They came back in the morning to ask for the return of the canoe. Even more remarkable, their request was granted.

As a result of concentrated work the provisions were ready and the ship fit for sea by 17 December 1773. Furneaux sent a midshipman, John Rowe, and nine others to 'gather wild greens for the Ship's Company with orders to return that evening, as I intended to sail the next morning'. The boat failed to return so next day, Furneaux sent Lieutenant Burney with a boat's crew and 10 marines to search for the lost party. Though at first they had thought that Rowe's boat must have gone adrift or been 'stove among the rocks' their suspicions were aroused by the behaviour of some Maoris they saw in East Bay. They rowed close to the south-east coastline of East Bay firing guns from time to time in order to locate the lost seamen. After turning into the channel which separates Pickersgill Island from the shore they began to see ominous signs. Beached in the bay just north of Grass Cove (plate 161) they saw a very large double canoe guarded by two men and a dog. The guards retreated hastily into the bush and Burney investigated the canoe. In it they found one of the rowlock ports of the cutter and some shoes which were known to belong to Mr Woodhouse, one of the missing men. Then they found about twenty food baskets which they cut open to find roasted human flesh and fern roots. They discovered irrefutable proof of the tragedy in Thomas Hill's hand—with the tattoo mark 'T.H.' which he had acquired in Tahiti—and some more shoes. There was also the circular pit which marked the position of the umu or Maori oven. Burney's

Plate 161. *In his search for the lost boat's crew, Lieutenant Burney passed through the narrows to the left of Pickersgill Island, in the foreground, and found the first grisly clues on the beach immediately beyond this passage. Grass Cove is behind the point beyond this beach.*

men noticed at this moment a great smoke from the next bay, Grass Cove,* and immediately pulled round the point for it was nearly sunset. Hauled up on the sand were four canoes—a single and three double ones—and there were a great many people on the beach. As the boat approached the shore the Maoris retreated to the hill, which rose towards the southern end of the beach and 'within a Ships length of the Water side', where they stopped to call out to the seamen. Burney ordered a musquetoon to be fired through one of the canoes in case it concealed any hiding natives and the sailors aimed a volley at the Maoris on the hill. A second volley caused them to scramble away as fast as they could, 'howling and hollowing'.

Courageously Burney landed on the beach

(plate 162) and with a small party of marines advanced slowly. The Maoris continued to retreat up the hill. 'Amongst the Indians were 2 very stout men who never offer'd to move till they found themselves forsaken by their companions & then they walkd away with great composure & deliberation.'

Lying on the sand Burney found two bundles of cut scurvy grass which had been gathered for loading into the cutter, and 'a broken piece of an Oar was stuck upright in the Ground to which they had tied their Canoes'. The party then searched the back of the beach to see if the cutter was there. They found no boat but instead 'Such a shocking scene of Carnage & Barbarity as can never be mentiond or thought of, but with horror.' There was nothing which could be done, so the search party moved back to the boat and destroyed three

*Now named Whareunga Bay.

128

of the canoes before returning sorrowfully to Ship Cove. 'The people lost in the Cutter were Mr Rowe, Mr Woodhouse, Francis Murphy Quartermaster, Wm Facey. Thos Hill, Edwd Jones, Michael Bell, Jno Cavenaugh Thos Milton & James Swilley the Captns Man.' At the ship they committed to the sea some pathetic remains— the tattooed hand of Thomas Hill, the hand of John Rowe, which was recognisable because of a scar on the forefinger, and the head of James Swilley who was a Negro.

Burney thought that the massacre was not a premeditated act but probably arose from some misunderstanding or quarrel together with 'our people being so very incautious & thinking themselves to Secure.' Captain Furneaux, who was a relative of John Rowe, decided to take his departure from the Sound as soon as possible.

Next morning, 23 December 1773, the *Adventure* unmoored and set sail, though she was not able to clear the New Zealand coast until Christmas Day 1773. Once out in the Pacific, Furneaux stood to the south until he reached the 58th parallel of latitude. Here 'the winds began to Blow strong from the SW and began to be very cold and as the Ship was low and deep loaden the sea made a continual breach over her which kept us always wet and by her straining very few of the people were dry in bed or on deck having no shelter to keep the sea from them. The Birds were the only companions we had in this vast ocean, except now and then we saw a Whale or Porpoise and now and then a seal or two and a few Penguins.'

The ship ran fast before the westerlies and passed well to the south of Cape Horn ('being in the Latitude of 61° South'), in just one month's sailing from Cape Palliser in New Zealand. Furneaux commented that in this run he had 'continual Westerly winds from SW to NW with a great sea following.'

By this time the *Adventure* was running short of provisions and Furneaux decided to make for the Cape of Good Hope, 'but first to stand into the Latitude and Longitude of Cape Circumcision.'

Plate 162. *A general view of Grass Cove from the air. Below lies part of Pickersgill Island, while the entrance of the Tory Channel into Cook Strait may be seen in the background.*

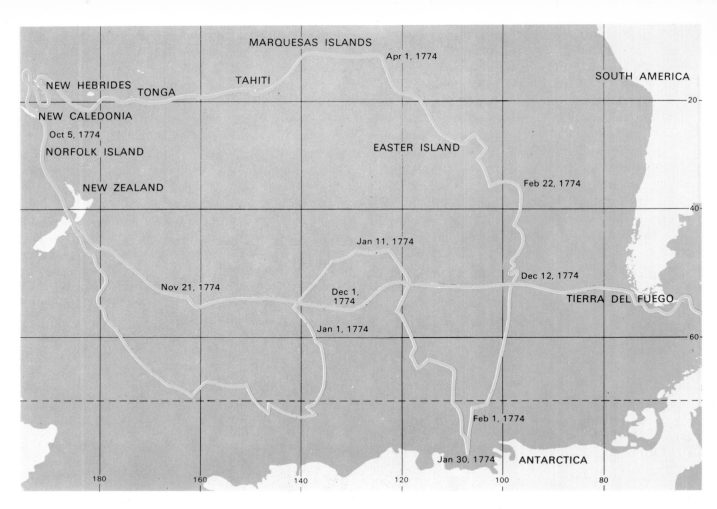

MARQUESAS ISLANDS
Apr 1, 1774

NEW HEBRIDES TONGA
TAHITI
SOUTH AMERICA

NEW CALEDONIA
Oct 5, 1774

NORFOLK ISLAND
EASTER ISLAND
Feb 22, 1774

NEW ZEALAND

Jan 11, 1774

Dec 12, 1774

Nov 21, 1774
Dec 1, 1774
TIERRA DEL FUEGO

Jan 1, 1774

Feb 1, 1774

Jan 30, 1774 ANTARCTICA

180 160 140 120 100 80
20 40 60

Plate 163. *Map of the* Resolution's *Summer Voyage. The comprehensive circuit through the South Pacific Ocean finally demonstrated that no "Southern Continent" existed there.*

It was still doubtful if Bouvet's discovery was part of a southern continent or merely an island set in most inhospitable seas. To the eastward of Cape Horn the *Adventure* ran into thick foggy weather which made navigation amongst the numerous icebergs a continuing nightmare. Though the seamen began to complain of the cold and pain in their limbs Furneaux persisted in his search for the cape. 'On the 3d of March being then in the Latd 54° 04′ South & Longitude 13° East which is the Latitude of the spot & half a degree to the East-ward of it and not seeing the least sign of Land hauled away to the Northward. . . . Should there be any Land thereabout it must be a very inconsiderable Island but believe it was nothing but Ice.'

As there was no evidence that Cape Circumcision was part of a large land mass, Furneaux sailed north to the Cape of Good Hope, arriving at Cape Town on 19 March 1774. After a month of refitting the *Adventure* sailed for England on 16 April and arrived at Spithead on 14 July 1774.

12   The Resolution

Nevertheless this shall not discourage me from fully exploring the Southern parts of the Pacific Ocean in the doing of which I intend to employ the whole of the insuing season

James Cook

Sometime about the middle of January 1774, the *Adventure* had crossed the path of the *Resolution* in the limitless wastes of the South Pacific Ocean. The same westerly gales buffeted both ships. Furneaux was running for the Horn on the 58° parallel and Cook was heading south again after having completed two legs of a giant south-north zigzag. The *Adventure*, with her decks awash, was no worse off than the *Resolution*, on which was George Forster who described the sea on 16 January 1774. 'At nine o'clock a huge mountainous wave struck the ship on the beam, and filled the decks with a deluge of water. It poured through the sky-light over our heads, and extinguished the candle, leaving us for a moment in doubt whether we were not totally overwhelmed and sinking into the abyss.'

Cook had made up his mind to steer south on this third leg of the zigzag, on 11 January 1774, much to the disappointment of his crew who had hoped he would head straight for Cape Town. John Elliott, the midshipman, wrote—'and many hints were thrown out to Captn Cook, to this effect; but he only smiled and said nothing, for he was close and secret in his intentions at all times, that not even his first Lieutenant knew, when we left a place, where we should go to next. In this respect, as well as many others, he was the fittest Man in the world for such a Voyage; In this instance all our hopes were blasted in a Minute, for from steering East, at Noon, Captn Cook orderd the Ship to steer due South, to our utter astonishment, and had the effect for a moment, of causing a buz in the Ship but which soon subsided.'

The 'buz' must have been a premonition of hard-ship because by 30 January 1774, the *Resolution* had penetrated far beyond the Antarctic Circle (plate 164) and had reached the amazing latitude of 71° 10′ south—further south than man had ever been. There was nothing but solid ice ahead and Cook had no option but to turn his ship northward. He wrote, 'I whose ambition leads me not only farther than any other man has been before me, but as far as I think it possible for man to go, was not sorry at meeting with this interruption, as it in some measure relieved us from the dangers and hardships inseparable with the Navigation of the Southern Polar regions.' These words written in his journal give a momentary and unusual glimpse of the man who wrote them.

This was a moment of climax as Cook was now certain that there was no southern continent in the south seas. Despite the theories of the geographers, despite the protestations of Alexander Dalrymple and the 'Continentalists', Cook, after 5 arduous years of exploration, knew that the Southern Continent did not exist—except perhaps in the unnavigable regions of the icecap.

It was decided that the ship would winter once again in the central Pacific and Cook set a course towards Easter Island. On 23 February 1774, he became very ill—probably with an acute gallstone obstruction and infection of the gall bladder. He was cared for by Dr Patten 'not only a skilfull Physician but a tender Nurse' and his recovery began when Mr Forster sacrificed a favourite dog to make soup and provide fresh meat. Those aboard were greatly relieved to see him improving as he had been near to death.

After Easter Island, the *Resolution* sailed on to the Marquesas and by April the seamen were tasting

Plate 164. *Far to the south, the* Resolution *sails past a tabular iceberg. A painting by William Hodges.*

again the generous hospitality of the Tahitians. Cook steered west again and after exploring the New Hebrides and New Caledonia he discovered Norfolk Island on his way back to New Zealand. He anchored for the third time, during this voyage, at Ship Cove, Queen Charlotte Sound, on 19 October 1774—just 3 months after Furneaux in the *Adventure* had arrived home in England.

It was with some satisfaction that Captain Cook found that the bottle, with the message to Furneaux, had been dug up from beneath the tree. His men also pointed out that some trees had been cut down with saw and axe, since the departure of the *Resolution*. The *Adventure* was safe and had survived the storms to re-enter Queen Charlotte Sound.

The aim was now to repair the *Resolution* with all possible dispatch, for the exploration had been completed and only the long run home lay ahead. The fore and main topmasts were unrigged, the

sails repaired or condemned and replaced, the hull scrubbed and the timbers caulked. While the seamen busied themselves with these tasks, others completed the gathering of wood and water. There was celery and scurvy grass to collect and fresh fish to catch. Mr Wales set up his observatory ashore and continued with his astronomical observations. Though Cook and the Forsters had some outings, in the main, the whole ship's complement concentrated on getting the ship and themselves ready for sea.

Cook, of course, knew nothing of the Grass Cove massacre but he noticed that the Maoris were timid and apprehensive. 'On our enquiring why they were afraid of us and for some of our old acquentances by name, they talked a great deal about killing which was so variously understood by us that we could gather nothing from it.' They sadly missed their interpreter, Odiddy, who had left the ship at Raiatea, his homeland, in

June 1774. However the Maoris soon regained their confidence and brought their usual gifts of fresh fish and implements. Some parties brought fine greenstone for barter and Cook mentioned that they acquired some of the largest pieces they had seen.

As always Captain Cook was interested in the fate of his farm animals. A sow was seen on Long Island, and the Forsters heard a pig squeal in the bush around West Bay. Cook put two more pigs ashore in the bay beyond Cannibal's Cove, now known as Waikawa. He was pleased that some of the animals were surviving and wrote, 'Sence the Natives did not distroy these Hogs when in their posession, we cannot suppose they will attempt it now, so that there is little fear but that this Country will soon be stocked with these Animals, both in a wild and domestick state.' He examined his vegetable gardens in various places, including Motuara, 'which we found allmost in a state of Nature and had been wholy neglected by the Inhabitants, nevertheless many Articles were in a florishing state'.

One question had been in his mind and he was determined to find the truth. When he had climbed the northern peak of Kaitapeha in 1770 and discovered Cook Strait there had been a stretch of water at his feet through which he had seen the tide running strongly. On 5 November 1774, he took the naturalists in the pinnace and rowed up the sound. Some Maoris had told him that this inlet joined with the sea so he made his way up what is now called Tory Channel to its mouth (plate 165). He found 'a large settlement of the Natives who received us with great courtesy' and examined the easterly sea entrance. The tide was flowing swiftly, so determining to make the most use of it he rowed back to the main sound, not having time to visit a large pa built on an elevation on the north side of the channel about a mile within the entrance.

The next day, 6 November 1774, was overcast with a little rain. An old friend known to the crew as 'Pedero', but whose real name was Matahua, had taken up his abode in Ship Cove and presented Cook with a handsome taiaha. He was rewarded with an old suit of clothes and a fine dinner on the *Resolution*. He ate well and drank a good deal of wine. 'Having got him and another into a communicative mood' Cook tried to find out the facts about the *Adventure*. He wrote, 'they gave us to understand in such a manner as admited of no doubt, that soon after we were gone, she arrived, that she stayed between ten and twenty days and had been gone ten Months. . . . This assertion and the manner they related to us the coming and going of the Adventure made me easy about her, but did not wholly set aside our doubts of some

Plate 165. *An aerial view looking across the seaward entrance of the Tory Channel, to Queen Charlotte Sound.*

disaster having happened to some other strangers.' Pedero was given an 'oyle Jarr' for his information, which made him as happy as a prince.

Once again Cook mentioned that the southern Maoris lacked the order and stability of the northern tribes. 'I am satisfied that the people in this Sound, which are upon the whole pretty numerous, are under no regular form of Government, or so united as to form one body politick; the head of each Tribe or family seems to be respected and that respect may on some occasions command obedience, but I doubt if they either have a right or power to inforce it. The other day when we were with Tringo-boohee, the people came from all parts to see us, which he endeavoured to prevent, he even went so far as to throw stones at some, but I observed that very few paid any regard to either his words or actions, and yet this man was spoke of as a Chief of some note. I have before made some remarks on the evils attending these people for want of a Union among themselves and the more I am acquented with them the more I find it to be so. Notwithstanding they are *Cannibals*, they are naturaly of a good disposission and have not a little share of humanity.'

Cook had an insatiable curiosity about the Maoris and recorded some of the more intimate details of their family life. Even after the *Resolution* had left Ship Cove, and was anchored in the sound awaiting a fair wind for departure, he returned to the shore to observe the natives. 'One little girl I observed was heating stones at a fire, curious to know what they were for I remained by her, for I thought they were to dress some sort of Victuals but I was misstaken for as soon as the stones were made hot, the girl took them hout of the fire and gave them to an hold Women who was siting in the hut, she put them in a heap and then laid over them a large handfull of green Sellery, over it a coarse Mat and then squated herself down upon her heels over all, thus she made what one may call a Dutch Warming-Pan on which she sit as close as a hare to her seat.' Cook explained that this may have had some curative effect. 'I should hardly have mentioned this circumstance if I had thought it had been done with no other view than to warm the old Womans back-side, I rather think it was done with a view of curing some disorder she might have upon her, which the Steams ariseing from the green Celery might be specifick. . . .'

Cook found the *Resolution* needed trimming so he ordered four boat loads of shingle to be used as ballast and struck down six guns, leaving only six on deck. They were ready for sea by Friday, 11 November 1774, the anchor was weighed and as the sails filled the *Resolution* glided from Queen Charlotte Sound—homeward bound. This time Cook decided to run eastwards across the Pacific in the middle fifties of latitude in order to quarter the last unmapped part of the ocean. Unknown to him Furneaux had followed a similar route, but a little further south. The *Resolution* made her South American landfall at Cape Deseado on 18 December 1774, and the crew spent the festive season in Christmas Sound in Tierra del Fuego. Captain Cook took his ship into the South Atlantic on 3 January 1775.

On still another cruise into the cold southern waters Cook found and explored South Georgia and then the South Sandwich Islands. But a further attempt to find Cape Circumcision failed because of Bouvet's misleading sailing instructions. The *Resolution* reached civilisation at Cape Town on 21 March 1775. Here Dr Sparrman took his leave to continue his botanical studies and the crew prepared for their return to England. They sailed from Cape Town on 27 April and arrived safely at Spithead on 30 July 1775. Captain Cook had much to report to the Admiralty and the nation.

He had done what he had set out to do. There was no Southern Continent in the southern oceans— though he postulated that there was probably land under the ice in Antarctica. He wrote with pride, 'Having been absent from England Three Years and Eighteen Days, in which time I lost but four men and one only of them from sickness'— and that not scurvy. Lind's theories had been successfully translated into practice. Mr Kendall's watch had exceeded expectations and Cook had proved a method which was to become standard for the estimation of longitude. The naturalists, not yet under the Admiralty's disapproval, had an immense amount of scientific data to study. The *Resolution* had proved a wonderful ship, worthy of her commander and crew. And Captain James Cook, who had surveyed New Zealand on his first voyage, had successfully used it as a forward base for his second expedition, during which he had virtually completed the exploration of the Pacific and Antarctic Oceans.

13 The Beginning

Today our Ship, which . . . might be called a second
Noahs Ark, poured out the Horses, Cattle, Sheep,
Goats &c. with peacocks, Turkeys, Geese &
Ducks, to the great Astonishment of the New Zealanders

David Samwell

The magnitude of Cook's success in his extraordinary second voyage was well recognised. His sovereign, King George III, eagerly sought an early interview with the navigator to hear, first-hand, of his explorations and to convey the congratulations of the nation. The Admiralty elevated him to the rank of Post-Captain and agreed to his application for a position on shore at Greenwich Hospital. He was honoured by the Royal Society who elected him to Fellowship and awarded him the Copley Medal for his work on sea scurvy. Wherever he went he was acclaimed by an adoring public. Captain James Cook, from a humble birth, had become the most famous and admired sailor not only in England but in the whole of Europe. It is hard for us, today, to realise his achievement in overcoming the social handicap of lowly birth in eighteenth century England to reach his position of eminence. It was a source of wonder to Admiral John Forbes, highly respected for his technical knowledge and judgment who paid this tribute to James Cook. 'He raised himself, solely by his merit, from a very obscure birth, to the rank of Post Captain in the royal navy.'

Now that Cook had solved the riddle of the Southern Continent, the Admiralty planned another voyage of exploration. For many years there had been stories of a seaway north of the American Continent linking the Atlantic and Pacific Oceans. This was the quest for the 'North-west Passage'. Search for this route in the high latitudes of the north would be a difficult and exacting task and one which would succeed or fail according to the qualities of the commander. All England, possibly including Cook, knew of only one man who could fit the post. Perhaps unwillingly, as he had looked forward to his shore posting and some family life, but probably inevitably, for this was the kind of work he was trained for and did supremely well, Captain Cook volunteered for the position. His application was accepted with unseemly haste.

Today the exploits of the astronauts in their journeys through space and to the moon are compared with Cook's great voyages into the unknown. One lesson mankind has learned in the years between is that enterprises of such scope and danger must be shared by many. One man, strained and changed by previous endeavour should not be asked to repeat his successes beyond the capabilities of human endurance. His past experiences and the mere passing of the years may rob a man of that flexibility and resilience with which he faces repeated challenge and adversity. Be that as it may, the assistance which the kindly fates had given to Cook on his second voyage, they were now preparing to take away. Even before the voyage started, when he was enjoying the acclaim of the nation and the warmth of family life, small clouds were gathering on the horizon heralding the storm which was to lead to his death on a distant island of the Pacific.

The *Resolution* perfectly suited Cook's requirements but she needed repairs and was sent to Deptford for this purpose. Whereas on her previous voyage Captain Cook watched the preparation and supervised the work, on this occasion he could not spare the time from completing the account of his second voyage. The refitting was undoubtedly done in a shoddy and disgraceful fashion. The *Resolution* leaked badly when she first left England, gave trouble throughout the voyage and the failure of her foremast rigging

near Hawaii led to the fatal decision to return to Kealakekua Bay. As consort to the *Resolution* a Whitby-built collier, the *Diligence* of 298 tons, was chosen. She was 'sheathed and filled' and converted from a brig to a ship—given three masts instead of two—and renamed the *Discovery*.

A number of the officers and men who had previously sailed with Cook joined this expedition. Two of them, Charles Clerke and William Anderson, were particularly close to their commander. Clerke (plate 166) was given command of the *Discovery* and Anderson became surgeon of the *Resolution*. Both were intelligent and educated men, both suffered from tuberculosis, both died on the voyage and by a strange mistake an island, passed on two different occasions, was named in honour of both. William Bligh, who later claimed his place in history by commanding the *Bounty*, was appointed master. John Gore, who had accompanied Banks to Iceland, rejoined Cook to become his first lieutenant, with James King, astronomer and journal-writer, as second lieutenant. John Williamson, who proved himself a difficult and head-strong young man was third lieutenant

and David Samwell, who wrote a most useful account of the voyage, was surgeon's mate.

With Captain Clerke sailed Lieutenant James Burney who had found the pathetic remains at Grass Cove. The surgeon's mate on the *Discovery* was William Ellis, mostly remembered for his fine bird sketches. John Webber was the official artist, William Bayly was again working for the Board of Longitude and David Nelson was the botanist, appointed at the request of Banks. In addition, Omai, brought to England by Furneaux, was being returned to his island home. The crew largely remain anonymous though one, William Watman, achieved some measure of fame by coming out of his retirement to serve Cook again, and by dying in Kealakekua Bay a short time before his commander.

The *Resolution* sailed from Plymouth on 12 July 1776, though Clerke was not able to leave with the *Discovery* until 1 August 1776. The *Resolution* called at Tenerife for fresh provisions and here Cook checked Kendall's watch which again accompanied him. The ships joined forces at Cape Town on 10 November and, after final

preparations, which included the loading of more livestock, they sailed on 1 December 1776, to begin once again, as Clerke had it, 'the old trade of exploring'. The first landfall was Prince Edward Island, the next objective elusive Kerguelen Island. The Island of Desolation seemed to Cook a more appropriate name because of the snow, the ice and the loneliness of that storm-girt place (plate 167). They landed in a bay which he called Christmas Harbour in honour of the day. Strong westerlies drove them on—and broke the foretop-mast and the main-topgallant mast of the *Resolution*—and Tasmania was reached on 26 January 1777. Three days later, not waiting to explore the coast or Bass Strait, Cook made for his old haunts in Queen Charlotte Sound.

The ships were anchored in Ship Cove on 12 February 1777. The sailors were greeted by the same dawn chorus from the bellbirds and the same mighty trees grew down to the shoreline. The few Maori visitors quickly recognised Omai, who had been with Furneaux at the time of the massacre, and realised that Captain Cook must know all about Grass Cove. For his part, Omai

regarded the natives with deep suspicion. However, the past was soon forgotten and the Maoris returned again with useful supplies of fresh fish.

During the next 2 days the observatories were erected under the control of King and Bayly (plates 168 and 169). But this time they had an armed sentry to guard them. Cook wrote, 'For the protection of the party on shore I appointed a guard of ten Marines and ordered arms for all the workmen, and Mr King and two or three petty officers remained constantly with them. A boat was never sent any considerable distance from the Ships without being armed, and under the direction of such officers as I could depend upon and who were well acquainted with the Natives.'

As the Maoris became more confident they collected at Ship Cove and built their temporary homes. Cook described the busy scene. 'I was present when a number of people landed and built one of these Villages: the moment the canoes landed men leaped out and at once took possession of a spot of ground, by tearing up the plants &ca or sticking up some part of the framing of the hut, they then returned to the canoe and secured thier

Plate 168 (above). *Ship Cove, Queen Charlotte Sound. An aquatint by Webber shows the two tents of the observatory on the south side of the stream. A group of Maoris watches while observations are being made under the protection of the marines nearby. The cliffs of Long Island may be seen in the background.*

Plate 169 (left). *A similar view of Ship Cove in 1969.*

Plate 170. *The Maoris, and their temporary dwellings, at Ship Cove. This water-colour drawing, by John Webber, gives a vivid impression of the Maoris' way of life. Captain Cook greets a Maori chief on the beach, with the* Resolution *and* Discovery *at their anchorages in the background.*

Weapons by seting them up against a tree or in such a manner as they could lay hold of them in an instant, I took particular notice that no one neglected this precaution. While the Men were employed raising the huts the Women were not idle, some were takeing care of the Canoes, some securing the Provisions, and the few utensels they are possess'd of, and others went to gather dry sticks to make a fire to dress their victuals; as to the Children I kept them, as also some of the more aged sufficiently employed in scrambling for beads till I had emptied my pockets and then I left them. . . . Mr Webber has made a drawing of one of these Villages that will convey a better idea of them than any discription' (plate 170).

In studying the Maori society Cook also drew attention to the family groups within the tribe. 'I observed that generally if not always the same Tribe or Family be it ever so large associated and built together, so that we frequently see a Village, as well as their larger towns, divided into different districts by low pallisades or what answers the same purpose.' These hapus or larger family groups were an important feature of Maori life.

The atmosphere of suspicion between the sailors and the Maoris had its advantages. The old friendliness had gone and the crew would not even consort with the Maori girls and women who made themselves so freely available. Cook was aware that such liaisons were sometimes a threat to their security, that venereal disease had been spread to the natives and that the attachment, in any case, was crude and insensitive—'how can it be otherwise sence all their View are selfish without the least mixture of regard or attatchment whatever. . . .'

All were determined to find out the facts of the Grass Cove affair. In this respect a tribute must be paid to the courage, or impudence, of Kahura, a powerfully built chief who was thought to have been the ringleader of the Maoris who caused the death of Mr Rowe and his nine men. Kahura and his family visited the ship with some apprehension expecting the justice he would so unhesitatingly have meted out to others. Captain Cook could not bring himself to judge the Maori by European standards, and wrote, 'Amongst those occasional Visiters was a Chief named Kahoura who headed the party that cut off Captain Furneaux's boat and who himself killed the officer that commanded. To judge of the character of this man by what some of his Country[men] said of him, he seemed to be a man more feared than beloved by them: many of them said he was a very bad man and importuned me to kill him, and I beleive they were not a little surprised that I

Plate 171. *Grass Cove, or Whareunga Bay, today. The sheep yards to the left mark the position of Rowe's boat. The party was having a meal near the stream, where the boatshed now stands. The hill in the centre of the picture concealed the Maoris, who rushed out on to the beach, cutting off the sailors from their guns in the boat.*

did not, for according to their ideas of equity this ought to have been done. But if I had followed the advice of all our pretended friends, I might have extirpated the whole race, for the people of each Hamlet or village by turns applyed to me to distroy the other a very striking proof of the divided state in which they live. We could not misunderstand them as Omai who understood their language perfectly well was our interpreter.'

There were two explanations of the events which led up to the massacre. Lieutenant Burney wrote— 'the best account I have been able to gather, is, that our people were dining on the beach: during their meal, a Zealander stole something out of the Boat, and was making off with it, on which Mr Rowe fired and killed the Thief on the spot. the Zealanders immediately sallied out of the Woods and got between our people and the boat. they say Rowe fired twice and killed another man, but the people's muskets had been left in the boat, nobody but himself having any fire arms, so that they were easily overpowerd and fell from imagining themselves too secure.'

The other account came from Kahura himself. He stated that 'on offering a stone hatchet for sale to one of the people, he kept it and would give nothing in return, on which they snatched from them some bread while they were at victuals.' The rest of his account differed very little from Burney's account and Cook pointed out that

Kahura's 'story of the Hatchet was certainly invented by Kahourah to make the English appear the first agressors'.

On Sunday, 16 February 1777, Cook set out with a party of boats to visit Grass Cove, the scene of the crime. He met his old friend Pedero who recounted details of the killing. He 'pointed to the place of the Sun when this happened, and according to it it must have been late in the afternoon: they also shewed us the spot where the boats crew sat at Victuals, and the place where the boat laid which was about two hundred yards from them with Captain Furneaux's black servant in her.' William Anderson recorded the exact spot where they sat down to eat, 'which is the corner of the cove on the right hand'.

Today, there is a boatshed at the head of the cove, on the right hand (plate 171). It stands about 200 yards south of the sandhills through which the little stream flows to the centre of the curving beach. A hill about 100 feet in height rises between the stream and the boatshed, its foot reaching almost to the sea. The ill-fated crew were having their evening meal at the right hand, or southern, end of the beach with Swilley guarding the boat near the mouth of the stream. When the fracas began Kahura called to his people on the sides of the hill and they immediately rushed down to the beach cutting the party off from the boat— and their guns. It is difficult now to imagine in this tranquil place those few moments of horror and fear.

Naturally, Captain Cook tended to dismiss the story put forward by Kahura—the accused. However, from this distance, there are some details which make one wonder where the fault really lay. There seems to be no doubt that the affair was unpremeditated, and all agree on this point. The explosion was set off by the actions of the moment. Rowe was certainly unwise and had been lulled into a false sense of security by the superiority of his firearms over the weapons of the Maoris. He was hot-headed as well as careless. On a previous occasion he would have killed some Maoris for theft had he not been restrained by the 'judicious and humane advice of Lieutenant Burney'. George Forster presented his view of some aspects of this young man's impetuosity. 'Mr Rowe, the unfortunate youth who had the command of this boat, combined with many liberal sentiments the prejudices of a naval education, which induced him to look upon all the natives of the South Sea with contempt, and to assume that kind of right over them, with which the Spaniards, in more barbarous ages, disposed of the lives of the American Indians.' It is also certain that Kahura would not have been slow to take offence.

The lesson to be learned from this tragedy was obvious. In the face of a large number of infuriated natives, willing to accept a few casualties, firearms would not be a decisive factor. Cook was well aware of this. He wrote, almost prophetically, of the natives, 'they were very sensible of the superiority they have over us in numbers and no one knows what an enraged multitude may do'.

Omai earnestly beseeched him to kill Kahura but Cook decided against revenge. Many times Kahura placed himself in Cook's hands and once sat for a portrait by Webber in the great cabin of the *Resolution*. Cook wrote, 'I must confess I admired his courage and was not a little pleased at the confidence he put in me.'

However, the urgent task of making the ship ready for sea took most of their time and effort. Damage was repaired, rigging checked and caulking continued for the *Resolution* was already showing signs of the slipshod work of the naval shipyards. Two men were detailed to brew spruce beer and parties, this time well-armed, collected greens for the crew and grass for the animals on board. Captain Cook went off to examine his gardens. On the Hippa Island, off Motuara, he found the vegetables growing, though still neglected. He noted that the ground was most suitable. 'The Potatoes were first brought from the Cape of Good Hope and have greatly emproved by change of soil, and were they properly cultivated few would exceed them.'

The little village had been destroyed but built again and contained about 30 houses (plate 172). Anderson, with a medical eye, noted that the houses were inhabited by fleas and that the village had two separate latrine areas—one at each end of the island. As there was no obvious water supply it was thought probable that the pa was not occupied continuously but was used only as a retreat in the face of immediate danger. To their surprise the party came upon the great timber post which had been placed by Captain Cook on the peak of Motuara when he made his claim for possession in 1770. It had been brought laboriously down the precipitous slopes of the island and hauled up the perpendicular sides of the 'Hippa', by some energetic Maori working party.

Meanwhile, Mr Bayly had completed a number of astronomical observations and had checked his findings with Kendall's watch. His estimation of longitude, $174° 25' 15''$ east, differed only slightly from the results Wales had produced—$174° 25' 07\frac{1}{2}''$ east. Some idea of the amount of work which Bayly applied to the determination of longitude may be inferred from Cook's statement, 'The Longitude of the Observatory in Ship Cove, by a Mean of 103 sets of Observations, each set consisting of Six or more observed distances is $174° 25' 15''$ E.' Both Bayly and Wales arrived at the figure of $41° 06'$, south, for the latitude of Ship Cove. These estimations confirmed the fact that there had been a slight error in the first map of New Zealand, and Cook wrote, 'it appears that the whole of Tavai-Poenammoo is laid down $40'$ too far East in the said Chart.' He was now confident of the position of New Zealand, 'for from this multitude of observations . . . few parts of the world are better ascertained than that of Queen Charlotte's Sound.' Modern maps are drawn in terms of Geodetic Datum 1949, so the measurements are accordingly 'geodetic' and not 'astronomic' and therefore not strictly comparable with Cook's estimations. Yet modern figures confirm the accuracy of the observations of his astronomers. The longitude of Ship Cove is now reckoned as $174° 14' 02''$ east of Greenwich and the latitude $41° 05' 44''$ south of the equator.

Plate 172. *"The inside of a Hippah in New Zeeland". This watercolour drawing, by John Webber, of the pa on the top of the "Hippa Island", shows in detail the construction of the Maori houses. Motuara and Point Jackson form the background.*

As always Captain Cook was very interested to see if the animals he had liberated were prospering. He felt the outlook was cheerful. 'I have at different times left in this Country not less than ten or a dozen hogs, besides those which Captain Furneaux put a shore, so that it will be a little extraordinary if there is not a breed either in a wild or domistic state or both.' He noted with pleasure that 'Poultry are now wild in the Woods behind Ship Cove.' He had meant to leave other livestock, including cattle, at Queen Charlotte Sound, but was doubtful if any of the chiefs had the authority, or the will, to protect or care for them. However, not long before the ship sailed he gave two breeding goats to Matahua, and a boar and sow to Tamatangi-au-uranui. He hoped that they would not be killed and eaten as soon as the ships were out of sight.

A young Maori lad named 'Tiarooa', who was well known to Cook from previous voyages, made friends with Omai and decided to sail with the *Resolution*. His father had been killed and his mother, though sad, raised no objection to his departure. To keep him company a little boy of about 10 years named 'Coaa' also came aboard. Captain Cook made it clear to everyone that it might not be possible to return these boys to their own country, but both were determined to go.

Tiaroa told his new friends about the Maori way of life which was dominated by the motive of utu or revenge. It was a duty to take affront easily and unpardonable to let an insult go unpunished. 'I am told that many years will sometimes elapse before a favourable oppertunity happens, and that the Son never losses sight of an injury that has been done his Father. There method of executing these horrible designs is by stealing upon the party in the night, and if they find them unguarded (which however I believe is very seldom the case) they kill every soul that falls in their way, not even sparing the Women and Children, and then either feast and gorge themselves on the spot or

Plate 173 (above). *A bellbird* (Anthornis melanura melanura), *painted by an unknown artist, on the* Resolution. *This, and the following bird painting, are in the Anderson Collection at the Royal Scottish Museum, in Edinburgh.*

Plate 174 (right). *The South Island kokako or orange-wattled crow* (Callaeas cinerea), *painted by the unknown artist, is probably now extinct.*

carry off as many of the dead as they can and do it at home with acts of brutality horrible to relate.' The myth of the 'Noble Savage' living at peace with nature on his island paradise, until brutalised by contact with the Europeans, must have received a severe setback at this description of the tribal customs of Queen Charlotte Sound. William Anderson had a satisfyingly simple explanation as to why the Maoris practised cannibalism, 'what originally gave rise to so barbarous a practice either in this or any other nation is perhaps hard to determine, but at present it would appear they do it merely for the sake of the delicious repast it affords.'

Visitors to Queen Charlotte Sound today see little evidence of the magnificent forest which once clothed the hills. The attractive coves and bays, the beaches and the waterways are still there, but much of the bush has been destroyed. Anderson's description tells us of its pristine glory. 'The quality of this soil is best indicated by the luxuriant growth of its products, for the hills (except a few towards the sea which are coverd with smaller bushes) are one continued forest of lofty trees which flourish with a vigour almost superior to any thing imagination can conceive, and afford an august prospect to those who are delighted with the grand and beautiful works of nature.' He also gave a detailed account of the birds which then thronged the bush—for instance 'a small greenish bird which is almost the only musical one here but is sufficient by itself to fill the woods with its melody, which is not only sweet but so varied that one would imagine he was surrounded by a hundred different sorts when the little warbler is near, from which circumstance we nam'd it the mocking bird' (plate 173).

Most of the birds have disappeared with the destruction of the forest. Some, indeed, are now extinct (plate 174). Queen Charlotte Sound, unlike Dusky Bay, has suffered grievously from the march of progress and civilisation.

143

Plate 175. *An aerial view of Cook's anchorage in Ship Cove, Queen Charlotte Sound.*

14   And The End

And no one knows what an enraged multitude may do

James Cook

On Tuesday, 25 March 1777, the *Resolution* and the *Discovery* stood out of Queen Charlotte Sound and made sail through the strait. Captain Cook had spent 100 days, during his five visits, in the safety and bounty of its waters. On a previous voyage George Forster had expressed the gratitude they all felt for its shelter. 'The keen air which is felt in New Zealand, on the finest days, contributed not a little to brace our fibres . . . and the strong exercise we took was doubtless beneficial in many respects. From hence it happened we always left that country with new vigour.' Cook now took leave of New Zealand for the last time (plate 175).

The next port of call was to be Tahiti where the animals were to be off-loaded for the benefit of the Islanders. Cook hoped for a fast passage as he still had 7,000 miles to cover before reaching the North American coast, where he had to arrive not later than June so that he could search for the North-west Passage during the summer months. But it was not to be. The voyage became a succession of frustrations and exasperations. It was as if Cook had, at last, been deserted by the fates. As he saw the coast of New Zealand disappear below the horizon the wail of a Maori dirge was in his ears. The Maori boys who had embarked with him 'gave way to their Grief by weeping aloud and singing a Song in a very melancholy cadence'. They were inconsolable for almost a week.

Adverse winds and calm weather prevented the ships from making an easting and they steered north to the Cook Islands. Realising that it was now too late for the northern journey, Cook conceded defeat and turned west for the Friendly Isles. He did much valuable work there before

gradually making his way eastwards to Tahiti. Throughout Polynesia pilfering and thieving by the natives drove Cook to distraction and he was at his wit's end to know how to deal with this problem. In desperation he resorted to harsher punishments, both for his own men and the Islanders. Some thought that these went beyond the point of just retribution.

At Tahiti he was crippled by what appears to have been a derangement of an intervertebral disc which must have caused him a great deal of pain, though he did not mention it in complaint. However, when 12 husky Tahitian women approached him to effect a cure it may be significant that he did not protest. They set about him pummelling, squeezing and twisting 'till they made my bones crack and a perfect Mummy of my flesh'. Their manipulations gave him some relief but would not necessarily prevent the return of the sleep-destroying pain.

From whatever cause, the severity of his punishments to the men, the burning of Moorean houses and the destruction of native canoes was behaviour quite foreign to his nature. Then, perhaps because of a changed atmosphere in the ship, a small wave of desertions began. One of the runaways, John Harrison, was tracked down by Cook, 'the Indians conducted our People to the House where he was & they found him lying down between two Women with his Hair stuck full of Flowers & his Dress the same as that of the Indians.' Harrison was, no doubt, surprised to see his commander and had to submit to being put in irons, and flogged. The situation was serious and Cook was annoyed and worried that his people would so readily desert him and his ship.

Plate 176. *The* Resolution *and* Discovery, *lying in Kealakekua Bay, in Hawaii, during Cook's second visit to the bay. The* Resolution's *foremast has been un-stepped and taken ashore for repair. An unsigned drawing, possibly by William Ellis.*

Plate 177. *Looking north across Kealakekua Bay today, from near the village of Napopo.*

He was distressed, too, that his men were taking venereal diseases to the Islanders. He tried to keep infected men on the ship but failed to do this effectively—and no doubt earned their enmity for trying. Already Clerke and Anderson were sorely ill and weak from tuberculosis. Anderson, the surgeon, was well aware of the progressive debility and inevitable death which awaited them and at one time thought that they should stay in Tahiti. But both were too loyal to leave their commander and decided to sail on until they died.

With such a background of anxiety Cook sailed his ships on to Hawaii, surveyed the iron-bound

coast of North America from Oregon to the Aleutian Islands, went on to spend an exhausting summer in the fogs and ice of the Bering Sea, but found no signs of any North-west Passage. He returned to the Hawaiian Islands for the winter so as to prepare his crews and ships for another attempt to find the nebulous passage during the forthcoming season.

Cook cruised off these Islands for 7 weeks, much to the indignation of his crew, before deciding to bring his ships to harbour. He had some unusually forthright words about the shoddy work that had been done at the naval yards at Deptford. The cordage and sails were rotting and the ships leaked badly. Resentful and harassed by these many worries he entered the rather exposed harbour of Kealakekua Bay, situated on the west coast of the island of Hawaii, the largest of the group, on 17 January 1779. The priests, leaders and the people saw in Cook's appearance a reincarnation of their god, Lono. They conferred their highest honours on their visitor and offered him gifts and adulation. But their devotion did not prevent them from stealing anything they could find. After refitting his ships as best he could Cook took them to sea on 4 February 1779, much to the relief of the islanders whose gifts and provisions were beginning to run short. Almost immediately gales struck the ships with great force and did serious damage to the *Resolution's* weakened foremast. Reluctantly Cook made the unavoidable but fatal decision to return to Kealakekua Bay (plate 176).

On his arrival at his previous anchorage Cook found the Hawaiians silent and a little hostile. Their pilfering reached new heights and there was obvious reluctance to part with their remaining stocks of food. One night the *Discovery's* large cutter was stolen and, with Clerke in no fit state of health to recover it, Cook himself took the necessary steps. He invited the paramount chief to board the *Resolution* as a hostage until the cutter was returned.

Large crowds of armed natives gathered on the shore to dissuade their chief from going aboard. At the critical moment news came of a shooting at the other end of the bay—but even then Cook's authority still held him safe against their mounting anger. At last, in a strange and desperate moment he fired a charge of small shot at one of his tormentors. The pellets rattled harmlessly off the man's thick cape so Cook fired again and killed a man. The wave of hostility then broke on the little party as a horde of enraged natives swarmed down the beach to the edge of the water and battered and stabbed until Captain Cook and four of his marines lay dead. Before the horrified eyes of the boat's crews they hauled Cook's mutilated body on to a little rock, awash in the newly stained waters of the Pacific.

Kealakekua today has changed little in appearance from the scene painted by Ellis in 1779 (plate 177). The tawny cliffs to the east still look down on the quiet waters of the bay. The shivering trees still crowd to the water's edge and the place where Cook fell. Napopo, a sleepy fishing village, still stands aloofly across the bay. On the northern shore the visitor may now see a rather uninspired concrete monument gleaming stiffly against the dark green shapes of the swaying coconut palms. Fifty yards further along the shore towards the cape which guards the northern approaches of the bay, is a small bronze plaque set in the seabed beneath the water (plate 178). Nearby is the rock on which Cook's broken body was thrown by the frenzied mob. Through the clear and gentle waves which wash over the plaque it is possible to read that James Cook died here on 14 February 1779.

Plate 178. *Beneath the clear waters of Kealakekua Bay this bronze plaque marks the place where James Cook fell.*

Plate 179. *James Cook, a cameo-portrait by Wedgwood and Bentley, modelled by John Flaxman in 1784.*

CONCLUSION

15 James Cook

*The ablest and most renowned Navigator this or any
country hath produced*

John Forbes

These are the proud words which Sir Hugh Palliser had inscribed on the monument he raised to James Cook, his protégé and friend. Britain's most famous seamen, Drake, Raleigh and Nelson claimed their position in wars which threatened the freedom of their nation and the generations they served. James Cook, pre-eminent in the arts of peace, introduced a new world to all the nations and to all the generations which followed him. What kind of man was this and whence did he derive his greatness?

His father was a Scottish farm labourer who, it is said, had moved south from Ednam, near the river Tweed, to work in Yorkshire. Here he married a local girl, Grace Pace of Stainton, on 10 October 1725, and the newly-weds set up their first home in the parish of Ormesby, nearby. After their first born arrived they moved to the village of Marton in the Cleveland Hills to work for Mr Mewburn, a farmer. It was here on 27 October 1728, that James Cook first saw the light of day. His home was a two-roomed mud-walled cottage with a thatched roof. When James was a week old he was christened in the Marton Church—'1728, Nobr. 3 James ye Son of James Cook labourer baptized.'

The Cook children attended the village school where they were taught to read and write by Dame Mary Walker, the schoolmistress. When James was 8 years old his father became foreman to Mr Thomas Scottowe, a farmer of 'Airyholm', near Great Ayton and the family moved 8 miles to live on the property.

It was a simple and frugal life in a harsh climate. In winter snow would sometimes lie for weeks and months at a time. The animals spent the colder months in barns and required feeding with root and hay crops. James must have worked hard at his many tasks because Mr Scottowe recognised his promise and paid for him to attend the day school in the village, where he was taught by Mr Pullen. The Postgate School still stands in High Street, Great Ayton, although it has been rebuilt since Cook's day. Here he was given instruction in reading, writing and arithmetic and seems to have shown considerable aptitude for figures. He also revealed a sturdy independent spirit which was described by his fellow pupils for the Rev. George Young, who published a biography of Cook in 1817. Whenever a class met to discuss an outing Cook would propose a plan, to which he would cling even in the face of opposition from all the others. In his spare time he acted as stable boy for his father on the farm.

By the end of 1744 there were eight Cook children and James, now 17, found a job as assistant to Mr William Sanderson, a draper and general dealer at Staithes, a small fishing town on the Yorkshire coast about 12 miles from his home. James had grown into a sturdy lad some 6 feet in height with an active and inquiring mind. He became fascinated by the sea, and in July 1746, with the blessing of his parents, he prevailed upon Mr Sanderson to take him to the nearby port and ship-building centre of Whitby (plate 180). Here he was introduced to Mr John Walker, a Quaker shipowner and master mariner, who hired him as an apprentice for 3 years, and became his lifelong friend.

Whitby, at this time, was growing faster than at any time in its history. Its 5,000 inhabitants

149

Plate 180. *The Port of Whitby today. A view from Cook's monument, looking across the River Esk towards the church, and the ruins of the Abbey on the hill.*

were crowded along both banks of the River Esk, which formed its harbour, in oak-timbered rough stone houses—though brick buildings were beginning to appear. The prosperity of the town depended on the coal which was mined in the vicinity and taken to London by a fleet of sturdy little colliers.

The Government had wisely imposed a charge on all the coal shipped from Whitby, and with the money thus collected was able to improve the harbour to give larger ships better access and more shelter from the fierce North Sea gales. Ship-yards sprang up along both sides of the river.

Most of the ships were built specially for the coal trade. They were of some 400 tons burden, and having a small draught, were able to work the shallow estuaries and harbours of the east coast. Solidly built to withstand the severe North Sea storms, they could be safely beached for inspection and repair. To man these ships young

men flocked into Whitby from the surrounding countryside, and at this time the town owned no fewer than 180 ships of over 80 tons burden.

It was in this booming port that James Cook was to make his home for the next 9 years. At the age of 18 years, in July 1747, he sailed out of Whitby as one of the apprentices of the *Freelove*, under Captain John Jefferson. He served the season with her until she was laid up for the winter. As was the custom Mr John Walker took his young apprentice into his own house and assisted him to learn the essentials of mathematics and navigation. In this he was helped by the housekeeper, Mary Prowd, who provided him with candles to study at night in the attic. No doubt John Walker's Quaker home provided James with some of his kindness and humanity.

After one more voyage in the *Freelove* James Cook returned to Whitby to find that Walker had launched a new ship. For 2 months he worked on it assisting to rig it and fit it for sea. On 14 June 1748 he sailed on the maiden voyage of the *Three Brothers*, as she had been named, under Jefferson once more. After completing two voyages in this ship, details of which are preserved in the Whitby Museum in the old sailors' insurance books entitled 'The Muster Rolls', Cook returned to Whitby on 20 April 1749. Here he received his first promotion to 'seaman before the mast'.

After 3 years at sea, at the age of 21 years, James Cook had learned much about the fitting and rigging of Whitby colliers. He had studied the arts of navigation and could handle a ship in the shoals and tides, and in the fogs and gales of the North Sea. Moreover, he had come to realise the strength and capacity of the Whitby coal ships which were the lifeblood of the trade. By 1752 he had become so proficient that the Walkers posted him as mate to their collier *Friendship*, and 3 years later he was offered her command.

Surprisingly, Cook turned down this offer and instead joined the Royal Navy. Here he would be offered the challenge of keen competition with the opportunity of advancement far beyond that of master of a collier. In 1755, he signed on as an ordinary seaman of the Navy. His first ship was HMS *Eagle*, under command of Captain Hamer, a ship of 60 guns, whose task was to harry the French in the English Channel. Within a short period Cook was promoted to master's mate and

then to boatswain. He was given the command of a little 40 ton cutter for chase and search operations off the French coast and he delivered safely to London a small enemy prize. By good fortune Captain Hugh Palliser was posted to command the *Eagle* in October 1755, and he immediately recognised Cook's powers of initiative and leadership. On his recommendation, Cook passed the examination for master at Trinity House in June 1757 and was went to HMS *Solebay* stationed at Leith. He was soon transferred to HMS *Pembroke* at Portsmouth as master under Captain John Simcoe, and commenced his duties on 27 October 1757—his twenty-ninth birthday. In February 1758 the *Pembroke* sailed with Admiral Boscawen's squadron to take part in the assault against the French stronghold of Quebec. Halifax was reached on 8 May 1758 but the crew was so weakened by sickness (29 had died of scurvy on the Atlantic crossing) that the ship could not reach Louisburg in time to take part in the landing.

As master, Cook was responsible to the captain for the navigation and handling of the ship. He lost no opportunity to learn the theoretical and practical aspects of this work, and while the ship was wintering in Halifax became intrigued by the mapping methods used on shore by a military engineer named Samuel Holland. Simcoe, scientifically-minded himself, encouraged Cook to find out all he could about surveying and it is easy to imagine

Plate 181. *The home of John Walker, built in 1688, still stands in Grape Lane, Whitby.*

the scene in the great cabin of the *Pembroke* as Cook and Holland crouched over the plane table discussing every aspect of the art. Here Cook learned the value of the 'geometrical' survey and was taught the use of the theodolite. It became his practice, when charting a bay or harbour, to establish a level baseline and to fix all further stations by triangulation, as visibility allowed. Cook soon had a chance to use his new knowledge and he charted the treacherous shoals of the St. Lawrence River with such accuracy that the ships of the Navy were able to carry the soldiers through waters hitherto thought unnavigable, to take by storm the heights of Quebec.

This brilliant work was noted by Admiral Sir Charles Saunders who, before he returned to England, ordered Cook's transfer to HMS *Northumberland*, flagship of Rear-admiral Lord Colville, who remained as commander-in-chief on the North American station.

Cook's next major task was to chart the coasts of Labrador and Newfoundland. He was given command of HMS *Grenville*, a small schooner with a crew of seven men, and for the next 4 years he crossed and recrossed the Atlantic to complete his survey. On 5 August 1766 he observed an eclipse of the sun from Burgeo Island off the south coast of Newfoundland where a cairn now marks his observation point. A paper based on these observations and the calculations of longitude made from them was presented to the Royal Society by Dr John Bevis on 30 April 1767. Thus the scientific world learned of the quality of Cook's work and his interest in the allied subjects of navigation and astronomy.

Towards the end of 1762 Cook returned to England and 6 weeks later, on 21 December 1762, married Miss Elizabeth Batts at Barking. They took a house at Shadwell, in London, and about a year later moved to Mile End Row to make their home. Their firstborn, James, arrived towards the end of 1763 but saw little enough of his father who spent the summer seasons charting the Newfoundland coasts, returning home to consolidate his work in the winter months.

Mrs Cook had a tragic family life (plate 182). In all, there were six children, though three of them died in early childhood. Her husband was killed in 1779 and her second son was drowned a year later when the *Thunderer* foundered in a West Indian hurricane. Her youngest son, who was a student at Cambridge, died suddenly in 1793 at

Plate 182. *Mrs Elizabeth Cook. Portrait by an unknown artist.*

the age of 17 years. The eldest son and the last of the children, James, was tragically lost near Poole when he was rejoining his ship, the *Spitfire*, in 1794. Mrs Cook lived on alone to a ripe old age and died on 13 May 1835, at the age of 93 years.

In the early years of their marriage, James Cook, then 40 years old, was ready to begin the work which was to make him famous. His vision and his qualities of leadership together with his years of training made him ideally suited for the great adventure. Having watched and guided his career, the Lords of the Admiralty confidently appointed him, in May 1768, to command the bark *Endeavour*.

When he was exploring the coast of New Zealand Cook remembered with gratitude the encouragement he had received from his senior officers who had recognised his worth and had helped him on his way. Some of their names are perpetuated in our majestic headlands. Cape Colville marks the northern tip of the Coromandel Peninsula. Cape Palliser dominates the eastern approaches to Cook Strait. Cape Saunders juts into the sea from the Otago coast and Cape Brett stands to the south of the Bay of Islands.

If the naval authorities were impressed by James Cook, those who worked and served with him fell even more under his influence. Cook, himself, revealed little of his thoughts or emotions in his writings and his personal letters were destroyed by his wife who saw no reason to preserve them for other eyes. But a living picture of the man may be pieced together from the words of those who sailed with him.

His appearance was described by David Samwell. 'His person was above 6 feet high, and though a good-looking man he was plain both in address and appearance. His head was small, his hair, which was a dark brown, he wore tied behind. His face was full of expression, his nose exceedingly well-shaped, his eyes, which were small and of a brown cast, were quick and piercing; his eyebrows prominent, which gave his countenance altogether an air of austerity' (plate 179).

Cook possessed the gift of leadership and his officers and crew served him with efficiency and loyalty. After the second voyage John Elliott, a midshipman, wrote, 'I will here do them the justice to say that No Men could behave better, under every circumstance than they did, the same must be said of the officers; and I will add that I believe their never was a Ship, where for so long a period, under such circumstances, more happiness, order, and obedience was enjoy'd.'

The accuracy of his navigation and the precision of his mapping became a legend. In addition to the 'geometrical' charting of harbours he perfected the 'running survey'. The speed with which he completed the mapping of the places he found is quite astonishing. During his first voyage, in addition to the 2,400 miles of the New Zealand coastline, which took only 6 months, he mapped 2,000 miles of the east Australian coast in 4 months. In his last voyage he charted over 3,000 miles of the intricate North American seaboard in a little over 4 months. When his survey of the Pacific Islands is added, he had drawn the modern map of the oceanic hemisphere and only a handful of the Polynesian islands remained to be discovered.

In each of his ships he formed a school of surveying amongst the junior officers and in this way his influence lasted for more than a century. Rear Admiral G. S. Ritchie, Hydrographer of the Navy, reminds us that Cook's methods were handed on to his pupils. 'Men like Vancouver, Riou and Bligh passed on their knowledge in turn to Mudge, Broughton, Flinders and others,

and thus we can trace through many lines the handing down of knowledge to Richards, Evans and Wharton at the end of the century, the original techniques constantly improved upon, with the dedication to accuracy unimpaired.'

Perhaps the greatest tribute to Cook's cartography was paid by Lieutenant Julien Crozet, an explorer whose life depended on the quality of the maps he used, and a Frenchman whose country was engaged in a struggle with England. 'As soon as I obtained information of the voyage of the Englishman, I carefully compared the chart I had prepared of that part of the coast of New Zealand along which we had coasted with that prepared by Captain Cook and his officers. I found it of an exactitude and of a thoroughness of detail which astonished me beyond all powers of expression, and I doubt much whether the charts of our own French coasts are laid down with greater precision. I think therefore that I cannot do better than to lay down our track off New Zealand on the chart prepared by this celebrated navigator.'

On his own ship Cook was absolute master and demanded instant and complete obedience. Unlike Abel Tasman he did not find it necessary to seek the approval of others or to devolve responsibility on to a committee. John Elliott wrote, 'he was close and secret in his intentions at all times, that not even his first Lieutenant knew, when we left a place, where we should go to next. In this respect, as well as many others, he was the fittest Man in the world for such a Voyage.'

When the occasion demanded it he could rant and roar and drive his men with the greatest vigour. Anders Sparrman described one such occasion. 'None but a seaman can realise how terrible was the sound of the waves breaking on the coral reef so near to us, mingled with the shouting of orders and the noise of the operations our dangerous situation made necessary. But even in my anxiety, I drew no small satisfaction from observing the rapidity and lack of confusion with which each command was executed to save the ship. No one seemed to be aware that he had been working for hours under a burning sun, the thermometer being 90° in the shade. . . . I should have preferred, however, to hear fewer 'Goddams' from the officers and Particularly the Captain who, while the danger lasted, stamped about the deck and grew hoarse with shouting.' It is hard to gauge the strain imposed upon Cook by such episodes.

Cook's nature was passionate but his temper was

usually well-controlled. However, towards the end of the third voyage he gave way more often to his anger and berated his officers and men, shouting and cursing and stamping his feet on the quarter-deck. The midshipmen irreverently called these sessions 'heivas'—noisy and threatening Polynesian war dances. These outbursts did not lessen their respect and admiration for him.

When his ship was safely in harbour Captain Cook managed to relax a little. He enjoyed his excursions in the peace and beauty of Dusky and Queen Charlotte Sounds. James Trevenen, another midshipman, accompanied Cook on such an outing—this one in Nootka Sound—'I with several other of our Midshipmen attended Captain Cook in this expedition, in which we rowed him not less than 30 miles during the day . . . Capt. Cooke also on these occasions, would sometimes relax from his almost constant severity of disposition, & condescend now and then, to converse familiarly with us. But it was only for the time, as soon as we entered the ships he became again the despot.'

The interest he had in science encouraged his artists and naturalists and their contributions greatly enhanced the value of his voyages and set the pattern for future expeditions. Thus Menzies accompanied Vancouver, Darwin sailed with Fitzroy, Huxley voyaged with Stanley and Hooker with Ross. Perhaps the first survey of New Zealand was the most complete and detailed ever made.

After the first two voyages his fame and reputation had become international. Though England was at war with France and Spain, these hostile nations gave instructions to their armed forces that every assistance should be afforded to Captain Cook. Benjamin Franklin, the American ambassador in France issued a directive to the United States Navy, 'you would treat the said Captain Cook and his People with all Civility and Kindness, affording them as common Friends to Mankind all the Assistance in your Power which they may happen to stand in need of.'

But though internationally acclaimed Captain Cook never lost his thoughtfulness and concern for his subordinates. This respect and humanity for his men is expressed time and time again in the journals and diaries they wrote. Henry Roberts, who sailed with Cook on two of his great voyages, put his thoughts very simply, 'such an able Navigator, equalld by few and excelled by none, justly stiled father of his people from his great good care and attention, honored, & beloved by those who knew, or ever heard of him.'

In his youth James Cook attracted the attention of those in authority who recognised his promise and his genius. During the two centuries which have elapsed since he first set foot in New Zealand, history has had time to judge his accomplishments. But, as a man, he is most clearly seen as a reflection in the eyes of those who knew him.

In New Zealand the passage of the years has hardly dimmed the mystique and romance which surrounded him. Perhaps his lowly birth, his rise to fame and his tragic and untimely death combine to stir and hold the imagination. In 1963 Lord Cobham, former Governor-General of New Zealand, wrote of Cook, 'New Zealanders owe this good man a debt of gratitude for the accuracy of his charts and soundings.'

He is indeed well remembered for these by our seafaring men. The senior officer of the Royal New Zealand Navy reveres Cook's memory no more than does the fisherman who shelters at Luncheon Cove in Dusky Sound, marked on Cook's map but lost by subsequent cartographers for 200 years. Captain C. W. MacIntosh of the fishing boat *Westward-Ho* helped to place a plaque in Pickersgill Harbour to commemorate the visit of the *Resolution*, but would accept no payment 'if it was for Captain Cook'.

New Zealand anthropology began with Cook's accurate description of the Maori people and it has served as a baseline for all subsequent research. Banks and Solander, together with the Forsters and Sparrman, laid the foundation for the study of natural history in New Zealand. The artists illuminated these accounts of the land, its people, its plants and birds.

His name will not be forgotten here. Joseph Banks named Cook Strait after its discoverer and Captain J. Lort Stokes of the *Acheron* suggested, in 1851, that our highest and most impressive mountain should be called Mount Cook. The Maori name is Aorangi—'cloud-piercer' or 'sky-cloud'. Its triple peak rises to 12,349 feet above sea level, soaring nearly 1,000 feet above its highest neighbours. It is a fitting memorial to Captain James Cook (plate 183).

During his visits to New Zealand James Cook formed a high opinion of the country and its inhabitants. He enjoyed the beauty of the mountains and the sounds, and admired the luxuriance of the vegetation. After 200 years his assessment of New Zealand still remains something of a challenge to

Plate 183. *The mists disperse to reveal Mount Cook.*

us. 'In short was this Country settled by an In-dustrus people they would very soon be supply'd not only with the necessarys but many of the luxuries of life.' He also wrote warmly of the Maoris. 'I have allways found them of a Brave, Noble, Open and benevolent disposition, but they are a people that will never put up with an insult if they have an oppertunity to resent it.'

For their part the Maoris revered Captain Cook for his bravery, justice and humanity. That quality which raised him above his fellows was recognised by the perceptive eyes of a Maori child who remembered Cook's authority and his kindness for the rest of his life. From the deck of the *Endeavour* as she lay in Mercury Bay, Te Horeta te Taniwha and his young friends paid the first and most truly New Zealand tribute to Captain James Cook, 'E kore te tino tangata e ngaro i roto i te tokomaha'—a noble man, a rangatira, cannot be lost in the crowd.

A SELECT READING LIST

Banks, Joseph. *The* Endeavour *Journal of Joseph Banks, 1768–1771*, ed. J. C. Beaglehole. 2 vols., Sydney, 1962.

Begg, A. Charles and Begg, Neil C. *Dusky Bay*. Christchurch, 1966.

Buck, Peter H. (Te Rangi Hiroa). *The Coming of the Maori*. Wellington, 1950.

Cook, James. *A Voyage towards the South Pole and Round the World, in His Majesty's Ships, the* Resolution *and* Adventure. 2 vols., London, 1777.

Cook, James. *A Voyage to the Pacific Ocean . . ., for making Discoveries in the Northern Hemisphere in the Years 1776, 1777, 1778, 1779, and 1780.* 2nd edition, 3 vols., London, 1785.

Cook, James. *The Journals of Captain James Cook*, ed. by J. C. Beaglehole. 4 vols. and an atlas of charts and views by R. A. Skelton. Cambridge, 1955.

Forster, J. G. A. *A Voyage Round the World in His Britannic Majesty's Sloop* Resolution. 2 vols., London, 1777.

Forster, J. R. *Observations made during a Voyage Round the World on Physical Geography, Natural History and Ethic Philosophy*. London, 1778.

Hawkesworth, J. *An Account of the Voyages . . . for making Discoveries in the Southern Hemisphere*. 3 vols., London, 1773.

McLintock, A. H. (ed). *A Descriptive Atlas of New Zealand*. Wellington, 1959.

McNab, Robert. *Murihiku. A History of the South Island of New Zealand and the Islands Adjacent and lying to the South, from 1642 to 1835*. Christchurch, 1909.

Naish, G. P. B. 'Cook as a navigator', *Endeavour*, Vol. 27, pp. 38–41, 1968.

Parkinson, Sydney. *Journal of a Voyage to the South Seas in His Majesty's Ship the* Endeavour. London, 1784.

Preston, C. *Captain James Cook*, R.N., F.R.S. *and Whitby*. Whitby, 1965.

Rienits, Rex and Thea. *The Voyages of Captain Cook*. London, 1968.

Ritchie, G. S. *The Admiralty Chart*. London, 1967.

Skelton, R. A. 'Cook's contribution to marine survey', *Endeavour*, Vol. 27, pp. 28–32, 1968.

Sparrman, Anders. *A Voyage round the World with Captain James Cook in H.M.S.* Resolution. London, 1944.

Stearn, William T. 'The botanical results of the *Endeavour* voyage', *Endeavour*, Vol. 27, pp. 3–10, 1968.

Tasman, Abel J. *Abel Janszoon Tasman's Journal*, ed. J. E. Heeres, Amsterdam, 1898.

Wales, William. *The Original Observations made in the Course of a Voyage towards the South Pole and Round the World in H.M.S.* Resolution *and* Adventure. London, 1777.

White, John. *Ancient history of the Maori*. 6 vols., Wellington, 1887–1891.

Williams, W. L. 'On the Visit of Captain Cook to Poverty Bay and Tolaga Bay', *Trans. N.Z. Inst.*, Vol. 21, pp. 389–397, 1888.

List of Plates

THE THIRD VOYAGE

JAMES COOK

Index

Proper names heading the main entries include those used by the early visitors, with explanatory notes in brackets and cross reference to modern terminology, for instance, Aeheino mouwe, *see* Te Ika a Maui. In alphabetical order, Te Whera comes before Tea plant. The subsidiary headings have also been placed alphabetically. The names of ships and systematic scientific names are in italics. We have used "n" placed directly after a page number to indicate reference to the footnote only, if separated by a comma the reference is to both the page and the footnote.

Acknowledgments

Two hundred years after Lieutenant Cook landed at Poverty Bay on our east coast we pause to remember the exactness of his survey of the coastline and the detailed records he made of the inhabitants, the fauna, and the flora of our country. In this age of astronauts and computers we can still look back to admire the human qualities which gave Cook his greatness. We remember that the primary objective of his first epic voyage was the exploration of New Zealand, and it was from his base in New Zealand that he subsequently charted the Oceanic Hemisphere. It is fitting that the New Zealand Government should set up a strong Cook Bi-centenary Committee to remind us of the debt we owe to James Cook.

It was this committee, through Mr C. H. Williams, Director of the Government Publicity Division, which gave us the daunting task of preparing a book to mark the occasion. Without the unfailing support and encouragement of Mr Williams and the great help of his staff we could not have met our deadline.

Perhaps it is no coincidence that the greatest authority on Cook and his times is a New Zealander, Dr J. C. Beaglehole. He has edited the Journals of Captain James Cook and Joseph Banks in such a complete and scholarly manner that there remains little for others to do. We have drawn much of the material of this book from Dr Beaglehole's volumes and we are further indebted to him for the foreword he has written.

Our thanks are also due to Mr W. S. Boyes, Assistant Surveyor-General, for advice and help with problems of surveying and navigation. In the design and preparation of the book the Government Printer's staff have spared no pains and we are grateful for their expert and constructive assistance. We are pleased to acknowledge the help of Mr J. D. Pascoe, National Archivist, who has taken a keen interest in the layout of the illustrations.

In an effort to relate the historical story to modern New Zealand we have followed by sea and by air the course of the *Endeavour* and the *Resolution* around our shores. We are grateful for the interest and the skill of our pilots who scurried across the sea at deck height or brought their aircraft down in the bays and harbours where Cook had landed. The launches on which we travelled were manoeuvred with great skill into unexpected coves when launch masters knew of our efforts to record the journeys of Captain Cook.

The text is drawn from the observations of men who took part in the great adventure and we have elected to illustrate the book with maps, charts, coastal profiles, and paintings made at that time by the artists and navigators who accompanied Cook on his voyages. These, of course, are dispersed around the world. We are indebted to the Trustees of the British Museum for permission to publish plates 1, 4, 6, 8, 9, 10, 15, 16, 17, 19, 20, 22, 24, 26, 28, 29, 31, 33, 35, 36, 38, 40, 42, 43, 44, 47, 48, 54, 56, 57, 59, 60, 69, 70, 77, 84, 88, 89, 91, 95, 96, 98, 100, 142, 167, 168, 172, and to the Trustees of the British Museum (Natural History) for allowing us to use plates 25, 30, 52, 72, 73, 82, 105, 119, 134, 135, 136, 137, 138, 139, 141, 150, 156, 157, 158, and 159. The Lords Commissioners of the Admiralty have kindly granted permission to reproduce plates 94, 103, 128, and 132, while the Director of the National Maritime Museum at Greenwich has provided reproductions for the cover, frontispiece, and plates 115 and 170. In London also, the Director of the Public Records Office has allowed us to use plate 176, while the Medical Director-General of the Navy has granted permission to publish plate 124. We are grateful to the Earl of Birkenhead for permission to publish plate 112, to the Hon. Mrs Clive Pearson, of Parham Park, Sussex, for allowing us to use plate 3, and to the Director of the Royal Scottish Museum in Edinburgh for granting leave to reproduce plates 173 and 174.

The Director of the Botanical Institute of the Academy of Sciences in Leningrad, U.S.S.R., has kindly provided plate 140, the Director of the Austrian National Library in Vienna, plate 113, and the Director of the Ethnographical Museum of Sweden, in Stockholm, has generously made available plate 12. The Director of the Australian National Library in Canberra has granted permission to reproduce plates 129 and 130, while the Principal Librarian of the Mitchell Library in Sydney has allowed us to use plates 66, 107, 108, 116, 118, 120, 121, 145, 164, and 182.

In New Zealand, the Governor-General, Sir Arthur Porritt, has kindly granted permission to reproduce plate 166. We are grateful to the Director of the Dominion Museum for allowing the use of plates 21 and 117 and to the Librarian of the Alexander Turnbull Library for permission to publish plates 2 and 86. The end papers and plates 109, 110, 111, 147, 152, 160, and 163 are the work of Mr E. L. Dyne, Chief Artist to the Government Printer. The Tourist and Publicity Department has provided plates 7, 14, 32, 37, 39, 41, 51, 53, 55, 92, 93, 101, 102, 122, 151, and 153.

We are grateful to the Librarian of the Hocken Library of the University of Otago for permission to reproduce plates 126, 127, and 179, to the Chief Librarian of the Dunedin Public Library and the McNab Collection for allowing us to use plate 114. The President of the Royal Society of New Zealand has granted permission to publish plates 11 and 13, and the Director of the Otago Museum has permitted us to reproduce plates 154 and 155.

Miss Evelyn Madigan has kindly provided us with plates 180 and 181. We are grateful to Mr Philip Dorizac for permission to use plate 143, to Mr Alan Seaton for the use of plate 64, and to Mr Barry Malcolm for providing us with plate 183. The remaining illustrations are from our collection: (A.C.B.) plates 18, 34, 45, 46, 49, 50, 58, 62, 63, 65, 67, 68, 71, 76, 78, 79, 80, 81, 83, 85, 87, 99, 104, 106, 125, 131, 144, 146, 148, 162, 175; and (N.C.B.) plates 5, 23, 27, 61, 74, 75, 90, 97, 123, 133, 149, 161, 165, 169, 171, 177, 178, and the back cover.

In Wellington, the photographic section of the Publicity Division of Government, the National Publicity Studios, produced and prepared many of these photographs for publication, while in Dunedin, we have had the benefit of Mr Alan Palmer's photographic skill.

The magic of Captain Cook's name persists in New Zealand and we have been greatly assisted by the many people we have met who share our enthusiasm for our subject. We wish to thank all these and in particular the members of our own families who have tolerated and accepted our erratic behaviour during these last hectic months.

Dunedin,
August 1969

A. CHARLES BEGG
NEIL C. BEGG

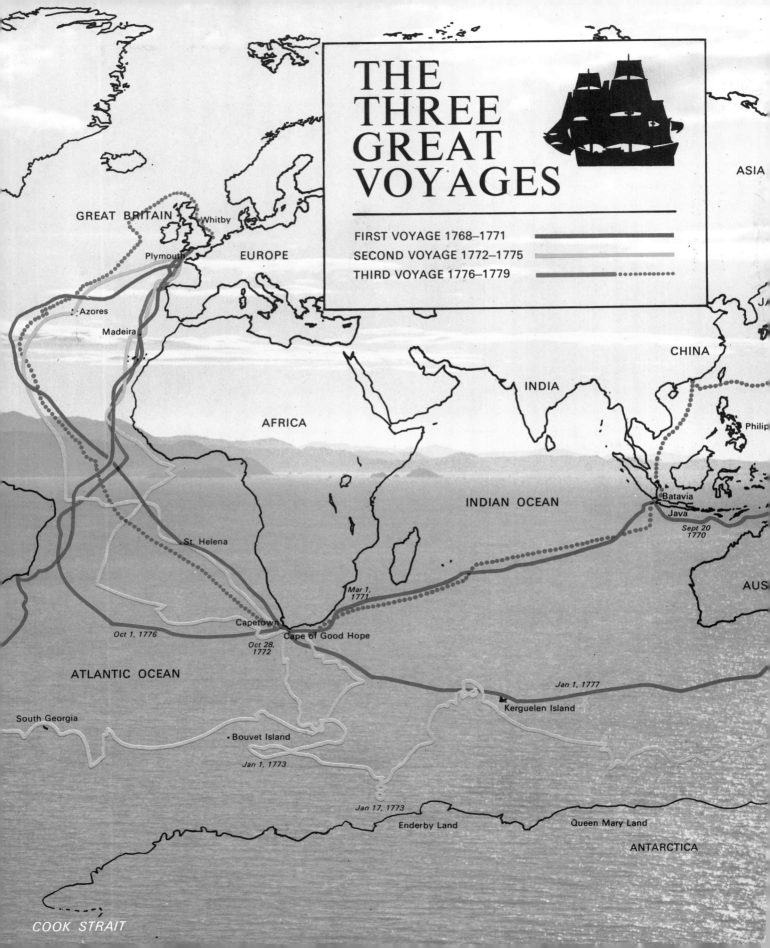

THE THREE GREAT VOYAGES

FIRST VOYAGE 1768–1771
SECOND VOYAGE 1772–1775
THIRD VOYAGE 1776–1779

ASIA

GREAT BRITAIN

Whitby

Plymouth

EUROPE

CHINA

Azores

Madeira

INDIA

AFRICA

Philip

Batavia

INDIAN OCEAN

Java

Sept 20
1770

St. Helena

Mar 1,
1771

AUS

Capetown

Cape of Good Hope

Oct 1, 1776

Oct 28,
1772

Jan 1, 1777

ATLANTIC OCEAN

Kerguelen Island

South Georgia

Bouvet Island

Jan 1, 1773

Jan 17, 1773

Enderby Land

Queen Mary Land

ANTARCTICA

COOK STRAIT